AWAKENING THE
WHOLE SELF

Timeless Wisdom and Modern Practices for a Balanced Life

HELEN SANDWICK

DEDICATION

To my parents, who shared an inquiring spirit to explore the world, live life to the full, never stop learning, and always keep a light touch.

To my sons, Raynard and James—you are my inspiration every day; I could not wish for more.

To my daughter-in-law, Linda - you light up a room with your positive energy and generous spirit; we are so lucky to have you in our lives.

To my grandchildren, Rio, Kai, and Ari - you tug at my heartstrings a hundred times a day.

To my sister, Christine - sharing our life stories and memories is always so much fun; love you loads and thank you for being my big sis.

To our wide circle of extended family and friends - thank you for your support and kindness over the years.

DISCLOSURE

While many of the Case Study characters are fictional and provided for inspiration, the places, travels and supporting literature are thoroughly researched. If a particular Case Study is factual, it is marked with an asterisk*. Visionaries are present-day innovators and real throughout.

Hopefully this mix of sample experiences, and opportunities for respite and replenishment, will provide you with fresh perspectives and a curiosity to explore and grow, as you move forwards in your personal Wholeness Journey.

DISCLAIMER

The information in this book is not intended to replace a one-on-one relationship with a qualified health care professional and is not intended as medical advice. It is intended as a sharing of knowledge and information from the research and experience of Helen Sandwick, and the experts who have contributed. We encourage you to make your own health care decisions based upon your research and in partnership with a qualified health care professional.

CONTENTS

CHAPTER 1

THE FOUNDATION OF HOLISTIC HEALTH

Setting Goals and Achieving Desired Results

When I first stumbled upon holistic health, it felt like discovering a hidden gem amid the chaotic world of wellness trends. Holistic health is not just a buzzword; it's a balanced approach that nurtures you physically, mentally, emotionally, and spiritually. It's like weaving together the strands of your life into a resilient and harmonious fabric. At its core, holistic health emphasizes the connectivity among all these aspects, recognizing that true well-being arises when each is nurtured. It is the ultimate personal development journey.

Intention plays a quiet but powerful role. Setting clear intentions helps you focus on balancing the different areas of your life. It becomes the compass guiding your journey toward holistic well-being.

In this chapter, we'll explore two inspiring personal stories that illustrate the power of intention and holistic healing, journey through ancient practices that laid the foundation for modern wellness, and conclude with a practical guide to help you begin your own transformation.

Case Study:

Stuart, Member of The Goldsmiths' Company in London, UK - Life-Changing Travel Abroad

Stuart, a member of The Goldsmiths' Company, one of the Great Twelve Livery Companies of the City of London, had masterfully navigated his role as an apprentice in his early years, later giving back through charitable efforts and mentoring promising apprentices. He loved his craft—the creativity it demanded, the strong sense of community, and the deep-rooted traditions of this 700-year-old organization. In his spare time, Stuart was an amateur archaeologist, delving into historical texts about ancient trade routes across global continents—this passion became his utmost fascination. In his formative years, he listened to inspiring tales from an adventurous aunt who once traversed the rugged Himalayas alone, in an era when that was feasible. This ignited a deep curiosity within him, driving him to explore further. He yearned for a stronger connection with these ancient lands, feeling as though his family tree had branched out from these roots and become lost.

Though he thrived in London's bustling cityscape, a yearning to venture to Tibet tugged at him relentlessly. Something resonated, and he could not let it go. Recently, he learned that a family in the Himalayas had opened a museum in Ladakh, a region where borders had shifted over time. Muzzamil Hussein had revisited an old generational property and uncovered crates stamped from cities around the globe, containing "silks from China, silver cookware from Afghanistan, rugs from Persia, turquoise from Tibet, saddles from Mongolia, and luxury soaps and salves from London, New York, and Munich."

This piqued Stuart's interest, and he decided to take a sabbatical from his London life to visit the museum, explore the region, and enjoy time to reflect and recharge. Following the trails of art, philosophies, and cultural beliefs throughout history would invigorate him and provide a fresh perspective. He learned of a wellness trekking tour between Lamayuru and Alchi Ladakh that would allow him to explore nature and several monasteries in the area. He would also visit archaeological sites, including petroglyphs and mystical caves used by both Buddhists and Shamans for their unique spiritual practices.

Stuart's hiking journey through the majestic mountains and his stays in serene Ladakh monasteries offered him solace and a striking contrast to the urban chaos he left behind. He embraced the monks' ascetic lifestyles, deeply rooted in spiritual practice and mindfulness. These experiences in rich historical settings catalyzed a profound transformation.

His daily participation in the monks' meditation and chants instilled a clearer understanding of life's interconnectedness through mind, body, and spirit. Tibetan monks, living embodiments of simplicity, taught Stuart the priceless value of being present and living in awareness. This journey reoriented his life, encouraging him to release past grudges and anxieties about tomorrow, grounding him firmly in the present.

Stuart adopted the monks' simplistic lifestyle—learning Tai Chi for physical and emotional resilience and appreciating the nutritional simplicity of meals made from local vegetables and herbal teas. This spiritual path represented a joyous return to authenticity, reconnecting him with himself while offering a broader cultural appreciation rooted in centuries of wisdom.

Stuart's story illustrates the power of blending modern urban life with ancient spiritual traditions, effectively supporting the book's broader message of holistic health. Upon returning to London, he infused his Tibetan-acquired insights into his daily life at The Goldsmiths' Company. By introducing mindful business practices and sharing his experiences, he inspired others to pursue their own creative and holistic health paths. His newfound appreciation for simplicity and presence didn't require abandoning his London lifestyle—instead, it deepened it.

Case Study:

Rachel, Currency Specialist in Hong Kong, China - Appears to Have It All

In the bustling landscape of corporate skyscrapers and power lunches in Hong Kong, Rachel stood out. An implant from New York City, she had pursued her MBA in the global financial space, expecting her stay to last just a few months. However, she discovered that this would become her career hub, her reason for professional existence in the coming years as the crypto space continued to evolve. She found it fascinating. Her life operated like a finely tuned Swiss watch—precise, orderly, and successful. Yet beneath the surface, she struggled with relentless stress and a growing emptiness. She moved through her days with every motion calculated for success. Ahead of the curve in the crypto space, she recognized the emergence of a newfound prosperity while others remained in denial, despite history's lessons. Between managing multimillion-dollar deals and maintaining a glistening social presence, Rachel seemed to achieve an almost mythical status. Yet beneath this veneer of perfection lay a soul grappling with the suffocating weight of unrelenting stress and latent emptiness.

Rachel's health, which had always been impeccable, began to falter as stress gnawed at her well-being. Sleepless nights became routine, her energy waned, and joy slowly retreated from her life. Externally, she maintained her polished persona; internally, she yearned for peace and fulfillment.

It was during a weekend getaway—a retreat she attended more to escape than to engage—where her life took a pivotal turn. Nestled in nature's tranquility, Rachel was introduced to the philosophy of holistic health. Here, in a serene environment far removed from urban chaos, whispers of ancient wisdom met the harmony of the natural world, igniting a spark that would alter her path forever.

In this sanctuary, Rachel learned about the interconnectedness of mind, body, and spirit. She delved into practices that emphasized balance and intentionality, starting with simple daily rituals that aligned her inner landscape with her external life.

Setting intentions became the cornerstone of Rachel's transformation. No longer just a vague idea, these intentions shaped her days, replacing her routine of relentless striving with purpose-driven actions. She embraced yoga and meditation, finding solace in rhythmic breathwork that anchored her scattered thoughts. These practices became not just exercises but essential lifelines, drawing her back to a state of centered calm amid the storm of corporate demands.

Rachel also reevaluated her diet and sleep, making conscious choices to restore her physical health and emotional vitality.

She began to view food as fuel for her journey, opting for nourishment over convenience, and explored the healing power of restorative sleep.

Emotionally, Rachel embarked on a path of self-discovery, connecting deeply with her inner world. She journaled extensively, uncovering layers of stress and imbalance that had previously masked her outward success. In these reflections, she found both clarity and liberation.

Rachel's life gradually transformed into a harmonious symphony of well-being and fulfillment. Her professional ambitions, once a source of stress, now harmonized beautifully with her personal fulfillment. She became a beacon of change, inspiring those around her. Colleagues noted her newfound serenity, and friends admired the soothing aura she carried.

Her journey serves as a vivid reminder that true transformation occurs when we align our lives with the rhythms of holistic wellness. In Rachel's story, we see that everything she sought externally, she found within—hidden in the simplicity of intentional and mindful living.

In the case studies, both individuals underwent transformations across all four dimensions of holistic health. Stuart's body strengthened through trekking and Tai Chi; his mind expanded through historical learning; emotionally, he released stress and connected with joy; and spiritually, he embraced deep meditative practices. Rachel also rebalanced her health holistically, restoring her physical energy, quieting her anxious mind, healing emotionally through journaling, and finding spiritual peace in mindfulness and purpose-driven living.

Just as Rachel and Stuart found healing by reconnecting with deeper aspects of themselves, today's holistic practices are grounded in ancient traditions that recognized this very truth. Let's take a brief journey through the origins of holistic healing across different civilizations to better understand their lasting influence.

A Journey Through Ancient Wisdom: Shaping Modern Holistic Health Practices

The evolution of ancient healing is a fascinating journey—from the mystical rituals of shamanism to the structured methods of Hippocratic medicine. Shamans employed spiritual practices to diagnose and treat ailments, while Hippocrates introduced observation and logic into healing. Together, they established a foundation that still informs today's holistic health approaches[1].

Archaeological and anthropological evidence has provided invaluable insights into many traditional practices, three examples of which are described below.

Ancient Egyptian Healing: The Temple of Imhotep

In ancient Egypt, health was viewed as a divine gift, often linked to spiritual and ritualistic practices. Among the ruins that whisper of Egypt's majestic past lies the temple of Imhotep, a revered physician whose practices laid the groundwork for many health principles still relevant today.[2] Imhotep, known as both a healer and architect, was deified posthumously, and his temple became a sanctuary for those seeking solace and healing. Patients flocked to these sacred precincts not only for physical remedies but also for spiritual rejuvenation, participating in rituals that combined medicinal herbs, incantations, and therapeutic sleep, embodying a holistic approach that intertwined body, mind, and spirit.

Ayurvedic Tradition: The Science of Life

In the lush landscapes of ancient India, Ayurveda emerged as one of the oldest forms of medicine, flourishing over 5,000 years ago. This holistic health system, outlined in sacred texts like the Charaka Samhita, emphasized a balanced lifestyle as essential to health. Central to Ayurveda is the concept of Doshas—Vata, Pitta, and Kapha—three energies believed to govern the body's functions. Achieving health involves balancing these Doshas through diet, herbal treatments, yoga, and meditation. Ayurveda focuses on prevention and promotes longevity by encouraging harmony with both the environment and oneself.[3,4]

Daoism and Inner Alchemy: Embracing Qi

In the bamboo-clad mountains of ancient China, Daoist monks pursued health practices centered on cultivating "qi," or life energy.[5] Meditation and Tai Chi were not just exercises but practices of internal cultivation—inner alchemy. These techniques aimed to align practitioners with the Tao, the natural order of the universe. By harmonizing their inner energy with nature, Daoists sought a life of balance, resilience, and peace.

Impact on Modern Holistic Health Practices

These ancient traditions collectively left indelible marks on modern holistic health practices, advocating for a multi-faceted approach to well-being that continues to inspire contemporary practitioners. The ancient wisdom of balancing the physical, mental, spiritual, and emotional aspects of health laid the foundation for what we now embrace in integrative health practices worldwide.

In today's spaces—be it through integrative medicine at hospitals, yoga studios, or wellness retreats—the echoes of Imhotep's sanctity, Ayurveda's balance, and Daoist flow resonate, reminding humanity of the wisdom of ancient paths where holistic well-being was a core life pursuit. These practices offer timeless wisdom for modern life, reminding us to seek balance in all areas of health as we navigate the complexities of the contemporary world.

Review and Implement

How can you take charge of your holistic journey? Start with physical health—commit to regular exercise and a balanced diet, providing your body with the nutrients, care, and rest it needs to thrive. Ensure restorative sleep and schedule those health check-ups you've been postponing, treating them as important wellness dates. For mental health, embrace stress management techniques and indulge in the joy of lifelong learning. Connect with others who uplift you, sparking conversations that stimulate your mind.

Emotionally, become attuned to your inner world. Recognize your feelings and learn to express them constructively. Surround yourself with relationships that feel like warm cocoons of support rather than complicated webs. Cultivate strategies to navigate life's challenges gracefully.

Spiritually, find that resonant chord within you that echoes with a higher purpose. Engage in mindfulness or meditation practices, approaching them as sacred rituals rather than chores. Connect with communities or cultural traditions that resonate with you, nurturing your spirit.

The next chapter will build on this foundation, exploring the transformative power of mindfulness in everyday life. By embracing these concepts, you'll uncover another layer of this intricate journey, progressing toward a state of balance that's about thriving in every sense. What small step will you take today to honor yourself and begin this beautiful journey toward balance and fulfillment?

Define Your Vision - Embark on Your Journey

Quick Checklist

Just like Stuart and Rachel's journeys—and the ancient practices that shaped their paths—your own transformation starts with small, intentional steps. Use this checklist as a springboard into your holistic health journey.

Physical Health

- **Engage in Regular Activities**: Incorporate exercises such as walking, cycling, or strength training to boost cardiovascular health and maintain muscle tone. These activities enhance circulation, elevate energy levels, and help prevent chronic conditions like hypertension and diabetes.

- **Balanced Diet**: Adopt a diet rich in a variety of fruits, vegetables, and lean proteins. This nutritional diversity ensures your body receives essential vitamins and minerals necessary for energy production and tissue repair.

- **Quality Sleep**: Aim for 7-9 hours of restful sleep each night. Quality sleep is crucial for cognitive function, emotional regulation, and physical recovery, enhancing overall mood and mental clarity.

- **Regular Health Check-Ups**: Schedule consistent screenings to monitor vital signs and detect potential health issues early, enabling timely intervention and ensuring comprehensive well-being.

Mental Health

- **Stress Management**: Integrate practices like meditation, yoga, or deep breathing exercises into your routine to manage stress effectively. These techniques help calm the mind, enhance focus, and improve emotional resilience.
- **Continuous Learning**: Pursue learning opportunities through online courses, reading, or engaging in new hobbies. This pursuit of knowledge stimulates cognitive growth, supports neuroplasticity, and encourages innovative thinking.
- **Social Interactions**: Build and maintain supportive relationships that offer emotional support and a sense of community. Healthy social interactions strengthen communication skills and emotional bonds.

Emotional Health

- Emotional Awareness: Develop awareness by identifying and expressing feelings through journaling or creative outlets like art or music. This practice assists in processing complex emotions and promotes psychological well-being.

- **Supportive Relationships**: Establish and nurture relationships that foster open communication and provide empathetic support, building trust and strengthening emotional connections.
- **Coping Strategies**: Utilize effective strategies such as therapy or support groups to manage life's challenges and enhance emotional resilience, ensuring a balanced and fulfilling emotional life.

Spiritual Health

- **Connection with Beliefs**: Seek a connection with a higher purpose or belief system that aligns with your values, offering guidance and a deeper sense of meaning. This connection can provide structure and hope in life decisions.
- **Mindfulness and Meditation**: Engage in regular mindfulness and meditation practices to cultivate spiritual growth and inner peace, allowing for self-reflection and stress reduction.
- **Community and Traditions**: Participate in community activities or cultural traditions to reinforce spiritual connections. These engagements can increase happiness, foster a sense of belonging, and strengthen community ties.

This comprehensive checklist integrates personal experiences with ancient wisdom, guiding individuals toward a holistic approach to health and well-being in all aspects of life.

CHAPTER 2

MINDFULNESS IN DAILY LIFE

Case Study:

Yuki, Marketing Manager in Tokyo, Japan - Overcoming Anxiety Through Mindfulness

In the heart of bustling Tokyo, Yuki, a dedicated marketing manager, found herself engulfed in anxiety. The pressures of meeting deadlines, delivering presentations, and navigating office politics left her overwhelmed and restless. Despite her outward success, Yuki felt trapped in a cycle of stress that seeped into her personal life, negatively impacting her health and relationships.

Determined to regain control, Yuki ventured into mindfulness, a practice she had only heard about in passing. Skeptical yet hopeful, she attended her first mindfulness meditation workshop. The calm atmosphere and gentle guidance opened a door she hadn't realized she needed.

Embracing mindfulness, Yuki began dedicating ten minutes each morning to meditation. Sitting quietly, she focused on her breath, observing each inhale and exhale as it flowed through her body. Initially, her mind resisted, darting between thoughts and worries. However, with each session, Yuki discovered a growing sense of inner calm—a space where she could detach from the noise and cultivate clarity.

This newfound practice gradually wove into Yuki's daily life. During stressful meetings, she instinctively relied on her mindful breathing techniques to remain grounded. Her ability to respond to challenges with composure rather than react with anxiety impressed her colleagues and began to reshape her professional interactions.

The most profound change was within Yuki herself. By reflecting on her thoughts without judgment, she learned to approach her emotions with compassion. The grip of anxiety loosened, allowing her to experience genuine joy and connection. Her relationships flourished as she became more present and understanding with those around her.

Yuki's story reminds us that even in the busiest lives, moments of peace are possible. Her experience demonstrates how mindfulness can help manage anxiety and rediscover joy in daily life.

Case Study:

Derek, Life Coach in Bethesda, MD - Mentoring Veterans Transitioning to Civilian Life

In Bethesda, Maryland, Derek has built a respected life coaching practice over the past decade, specializing in helping military personnel transition to civilian life. Recognizing their unique struggles, he incorporates mindfulness into his coaching, offering positivity and presence as calming contrasts to painful memories. Derek observes significant stress reduction and improved emotional well-being among his veteran clients.

Transformative Techniques

Every morning, Derek practices mindfulness meditation to maintain his balance, ensuring he brings clarity and empathy into each coaching interaction. He begins each day in early-morning silence, centering himself with mindful breathing before meeting clients.

Within his sessions, Derek uses mindfulness not just as a tool but as a philosophy. He teaches mindful listening, enabling veterans to process emotions with patience—a necessary skill as they navigate their new lives. These practices, coupled with breathing exercises, help them find peace amid anxiety.

Derek emphasizes the power of mindfulness through shared experiences, encouraging veterans to support one another in group settings. This community aspect fosters a collective healing atmosphere, crucial for individuals who thrive in structured teamwork environments.

Challenges and Discoveries

Despite initial skepticism from some clients regarding meditation's benefits, Derek's perseverance yields positive results. His patient guidance helps many embrace mindfulness, unlocking new ways to manage anxiety and rediscover confidence.

Impactful Outcomes

Over time, Derek has witnessed his clients achieve significant milestones—improved focus, better emotional regulation, and renewed confidence. These outcomes motivate Derek, confirming the value of mindfulness beyond theoretical benefits.

His dedication not only enhances his clients' lives but also enriches the local veteran community, fostering a ripple effect of wellness throughout the area. Through mindfulness, Derek empowers his clients to view change not as a challenge but as an opportunity for growth and peace. His story highlights mindfulness's impact on personal transformation, illustrating its role in aiding life's transitions with grace and resilience.

Just as Derek's clients find peace in the present, they tap into practices that originated thousands of years ago, showing how mindfulness remains as vital today as it was in ancient times.

Mindfulness in Ancient Buddhist Practices

In the serene and remote region of what is now Nepal, during the 5th century BCE, a prince named Siddhartha Gautama embarked on a journey that would later change the world [1]. As the founder of Buddhism, Siddhartha, later known as the Buddha, pioneered mindfulness practices that are still revered today.

Mindfulness, or "sati" in Pali, was central to the Buddha's teachings, representing an awareness of the present moment that encompasses body, feelings, mind, and phenomena. This practice was not merely a meditative exercise but a way of living that embraced clarity, understanding, and peace.

During his teaching period in the deer park at Sarnath, the Buddha introduced the Satipatthana Sutta, a guide to the four foundations of mindfulness, which instructed followers to observe their thoughts, feelings, and bodily sensations with full attention and calm awareness.[2]

Amidst the quietude of monastic life, practitioners sat in silent meditation, their minds attentively following their breath, noting each inhalation and exhalation. The scenery—a world of rustling leaves, bird songs, and distant chants—enhanced the atmosphere of peace and reflection.

In this environment, mindfulness became a practice of awakening, a meticulous observation that led to insights into the nature of suffering and the path to bliss.

This historical context highlights how mindfulness was more than a technique for relaxation or focus. For ancient Buddhists, it was a path to inner freedom—an essential part of the journey to release suffering and discover lasting peace. Today, the Buddha's teachings on mindfulness continue to resonate globally, showcasing the timeless and universal appeal of this practice.

Mindfulness in Our Modern World

In the early 2000s, a small Pennsylvania-based company named Rodale Inc., known for its focus on wellness and lifestyle, embarked on a journey closely mirroring the principles of Siddhartha Gautama's mindfulness practices.

Established in 1930, Rodale initially specialized in promoting healthy living through various publications, such as *Men's Health* and *Women's Health*. However, it was their organic farming and gardening guide, *Organic Gardening*, that truly set them apart. This was the seed of a business movement that became synonymous with balance and holistic living.

Rodale Inc. pioneered sustainable and holistic business practices long before wellness became a mainstream focus. By integrating mindfulness principles into its operations—

acting with intention, aligning with nature, and fostering well-being in everyday life—these values became the heart of its business ethos. This approach not only echoes the teachings of Siddhartha Gautama but also demonstrates a successful business shift toward holistic wellness. Although the company was eventually sold to Hearst in 2017, its legacy continues to impact the wellness and lifestyle sectors.[3]

Eight Science-Backed Ways Mindfulness Helps Us Heal and Thrive

1. Burnout

The article by Janssen et al. provides a systematic review of the effects of Mindfulness-Based Stress Reduction (MBSR) on employees' mental health, specifically focusing on burnout. The review finds that MBSR can significantly reduce symptoms of burnout among employees by fostering greater emotional resilience and improving stress management skills. Employees practicing mindfulness report better mental health, indicating the beneficial role mindfulness plays in mitigating occupational stress and emotional exhaustion.[4]

2. Addiction

The article by Zhang et al. reviews the effectiveness of mindfulness-based interventions on various health outcomes, including addiction. It highlights how mindfulness practices can help reduce addictive behaviors by increasing self-awareness and decreasing cravings. Mindfulness-based interventions are shown to interrupt the automaticity of addictive responses, allowing individuals to respond more intentionally to triggers.[5]

3. Emotional Hopelessness

An article by Lu et al. discusses how mindfulness-based interventions can effectively reduce stress, a key contributor to hopelessness and suicidal tendencies. These practices equip individuals with tools to better manage stress and cope with suicidal thoughts by fostering self-awareness and emotional regulation. Such interventions cultivate resilience and mitigate risk factors associated with suicide.[6]

4. Bias/Harassment

Lueke and Gibson explore the effects of mindfulness meditation on implicit age and race bias. Their study suggests that mindfulness reduces bias by diminishing the automaticity of responses that often lead to discriminatory behavior. By enhancing awareness and control over reflexive judgments, mindfulness promotes more deliberate and equitable interactions.[7]

5. Team Dynamics

The research by Liu et al. examines how individual and team mindfulness impacts work engagement. Findings indicate that mindfulness at both levels enhances team dynamics by improving communication, alleviating work-related stress, and fostering a collaborative work environment. This results in greater work engagement and improved team performance.[8]

6. Worker and Personal Productivity

He, Li, Wang, and Xu's study investigates the relationship between mindfulness and work performance, specifically among web editors. It highlights that mindfulness boosts productivity by fostering workplace spirituality and enhancing digital competencies. These elements lead to improved focus, better stress management, and more effective task handling, ultimately increasing worker and personal productivity.9

7. Focus/Attention

The article by Prakash et al. reviews the impact of mindfulness on attention, outlining current research and future directions. It emphasizes that mindfulness practices enhance attentional control and cognitive performance by promoting greater focus and reducing distractions. This improved capacity allows individuals to maintain sustained attention on tasks and manage their cognitive resources more effectively.[10]

8. Creativity/Innovation

The research by Capurso, Fabbro, and Crescentini investigates how mindfulness meditation influences creative thinking. The study indicates that mindfulness enhances creativity by fostering cognitive flexibility and openness to new ideas. It suggests that mindfulness meditation enables individuals to approach problems from fresh perspectives, facilitating innovative solutions and creative processes.11

Key Benefits	Mindfulness Categories
Enhanced Awareness	Bias/Harassment
Enhanced Digital Competencies	Productivity
Enhanced Mental Health	Burnout, Emotional Hopelessness
Enhanced Openness to Ideas	Creativity/Innovation
Improved Communication	Team Dynamics
Improved Emotional Regulation	Addiction, Emotional Hopelessness
Improved Focus	Productivity, Focus/Attention
Improved Stress Management	Burnout, Emotional Hopelessness, Addiction, Team Dynamics, Productivity
Increased Cognitive Flexibility	Creativity/Innovation
Increased Emotional Resilience	Burnout, Emotional Hopelessness
Increased Self-Awareness	Addiction, Emotional Hopelessness
Reduced Cravings	Addiction
Reduced Emotional Exhaustion	Burnout, Emotional Hopelessness
Reduced Implicit Bias	Bias/Harassment

Review and Implement

At the heart of mindfulness lies a powerful truth: it's about engaging deeply with the present moment, letting go of judgments, and finding tranquility within. Contrary to some misconceptions, mindfulness doesn't require us to erase our thoughts or escape to a serene mountaintop—though retreats can be refreshing. Instead, it invites us to integrate awareness into our daily activities, right here and now. To incorporate mindfulness into your life, start with a simple exercise from the checklist below.

Chart Your Path - Ignite Your Progress

Quick Checklist

Two-Minute Breathing Technique

1. Find a comfortable seated position.
2. Close your eyes and take a deep breath in through your nose, fully filling your lungs.
3. Hold your breath for a count of three.
4. Exhale slowly through your mouth, feeling tension release.
5. Repeat this cycle for two minutes, focusing on the sensation of your breath.

Step-by-Step Mindfulness Exercise (Under Five Minutes)

1. **Find a Quiet Spot:** Sit comfortably with your back straight and hands resting on your lap.

2. **Ground Yourself:** Notice any physical sensations, starting from your feet and moving upwards.

3. **Focus on Your Breath:** Close your eyes and take a deep breath, paying attention to the rise and fall of your chest.

4. **Be Aware of Thoughts:** Acknowledge any thoughts that arise without judgment, then gently redirect your attention back to your breath.

5. **Return to Calmness:** After five minutes, take a final deep breath and open your eyes, feeling refreshed and centered.

The immediate benefit of these exercises is a sense of calm and centeredness, reducing stress and enhancing focus.

Do you enjoy reflecting through writing? After your mindfulness practice, consider journaling about your observations—your breath, your thoughts, or how you felt. It's a simple way to deepen self-awareness and track your journey.

As we explore the principles of mindfulness rooted in ancient Buddhist practices, we naturally transition to meditation—a practice that beautifully arises from these principles. Meditation is not merely an extension of mindfulness; it embodies its essence, offering a deeper exploration of awareness and tranquility. This practice builds on the foundation laid by mindfulness and elevates it to a state of stillness and reflection, inviting you to explore the inner land-scapes of your mind on a journey toward enlightenment and peace.

Are you ready to explore the next layer of your journey? In the coming chapter, we'll delve into the heart of mindful-ness—meditation—and discover how it can bring even greater calm and clarity to your everyday life.

CHAPTER 3

MEDITATION TECHNIQUES FOR MODERN LIVING

Case Study:

Daniel, Principal Broker in Paris, France - Personal Growth and Transformation in Zambia

Daniel, a former principal real estate broker with offices across New York, London, Paris, Dubai, Cape Town, and Hong Kong, had long sought relief from his high-stakes lifestyle. An American based in Paris, he reached out to the Peace Corps and learned about an opportunity in Zambia with the Linking Income Food and Environment (LIFE) Project[1].

This opportunity resonated deeply with him, prompting him to begin planning for a smooth transfer of knowledge to his business partners and key team members before his departure.

During his two-year involvement in Zambia, Daniel worked to enhance food security and expand economic opportunities in the region, experiences that profoundly transformed him. Captivated by the country and its people, he felt a sense of grounding and connection with his true self like never before. Hesitant to return to Paris after his tour, he chose to extend his stay in Africa, dedicating time to unwind and reflect on the past several months and his future direction.

Daniel had always dreamed of going on a safari. He viewed it as the perfect opportunity to embark on a personal inner journey while embracing the essence of African meditation, which centers around spiritual connection and harmony. In his quest for the ideal experience, Daniel discovered a wellness safari that traversed Zambia and Botswana, fitting seamlessly into his plans.[2]

Wilderness Toka Leya

The safari began with a three-night stay at Wilderness Toka Leya in Livingstone, Zambia. Nestled on the banks of the Zambezi River and near the vibrant activities of Victoria Falls, yet isolated enough for a true bush experience, the camp provided an ideal setting for Daniel to deepen his meditation and reflection.

It allowed him to savor simple tent life with offerings of yoga and meditation at the wellness center. This environment facilitated his reconnection with nature through serene activities like boating and fishing. The thrill of game drives and rhino tracking contrasted with tranquil bird watching and guided walks. A key highlight was the overnight drive through the wilderness to witness leopards in their natural habitat, a memory Daniel and his fellow travelers would cherish forever.

Surrounded by untamed beauty, Daniel felt his spirit rejuvenated, marking the first steps of a journey of self-discovery intertwined with Africa's wild rhythms.

Wilderness Duma Tau

Next on the agenda was a light aircraft transfer from Kasane Airport to Wilderness Duma Tau in Linyanti, Botswana. Here, the group set out in a quiet, eco-friendly safari vehicle designed to immerse guests in nature while minimizing their carbon footprint.[3] Staying in eco-friendly tents with spectacular, panoramic views of the wildlife-rich Osprey Lagoon, he was inspired by the sight of mega-herds of elephants passing by, stopping briefly to munch on waterlilies. A helicopter ride over the area and a barge trip along the waterways provided new perspectives, followed by an unparalleled outdoor dining experience.[4]

The Night Drive offered a chance to spot elusive nocturnal animals under a spectacular ink-navy sky sprinkled with an infinite universe of glistening stars. The air was cool, crisp, and clear. Daniel was fortunate to capture unique photographic moments of bushbabies, spotted genets, and even an extremely rare sighting of a pangolin.[5]

Watching wildlife just a few feet away from the game viewing hide—herds of buffalo and elephants, lions and wild dogs stalking their prey—deepened his connection with nature.

On the final evening, Daniel opted for quiet time at the spa, relaxed in the plunge pool, and shared stories around the floating firepit with his newfound friends. They savored the chef's specialties while listening to the occasional hoot of an owl in the distance, watching the sun set against the evening sky. These moments, enriched by nature's beauty and camaraderie, supported his meditation and personal transformation, paving the way for his evolving journey.

Wilderness Jao

In the early morning, Daniel and his group flew to Wilderness Jao, a remote island in Okavango, Botswana, for the final three days.

Here, he felt a mix of emotions—regret that the journey was ending and restlessness from the new creative energy rising within him. Meditation and distance from worldly concerns had taken root, and Daniel was ready to dream again.

Jao's expansive 60,000-hectare reserve, with its lush islands bordered by tributary forests and vast floodplains, offered panoramic views and moments of reflection from the private sala (open balcony). Guests could enjoy afternoon siestas or simply take in the ambiance. For the curious, a library beckoned them to explore literature that resonated with their experiences at this unique camp.

Conversations with a San guide led to a special invitation to the Tsodilo Hills, a place steeped in history and now a UNESCO site. With prior approval from the elders, the guide felt honored to take the group to visit this sacred location.[6]

During the drive, stories were shared about the San people, who date back 70,000 years. They were the first to stand upright, speak a language, make tools, and control fire. Later, as they migrated, they shared their knowledge and explored new territories. Their DNA can be linked to nearly all populations in the world.[7] These stories of exploration and knowledge resonated deeply with Daniel and mirrored his newfound sense of purpose.

San Bushmen

In this highly spiritual place, one of the oldest historical sites on earth, they explored rock art, paintings, and engravings depicting the daily life and spiritual beliefs of the San people. The four main hills—Male, Female, Child, and Leaning Rock—are deeply significant for the San as sites for sacred rituals. Here, they engage in vibrant dances and storytelling, venerating the python, from which they believe mankind descended. Guidance and healing from the spirit world, along with balance with nature, are key aspects of their belief system. The personalized experience was incredible, and the group thanked the San guide and his colleagues for this surprise trip that they would remember forever.[8,9]

Back at base the next day, Daniel journeyed along the reed-fringed waterways in a glass-bottomed mokoro (dugout canoe), listening with a hint of trepidation for hippopotamus grunts and other wildlife.[10] As the seasoned polers guided the mokoros along, he enjoyed sightings of giraffes, zebras, wildebeests, and local elephants. The evening brought a medley of traditional food, song, and dance at the boma (communal space).

Choosing the Star Bed experience, Daniel cherished the distant sounds of nature—hyenas, jackals, and lions—each wrestling with the night's adventures and choosing resting places with vigilance.[11]

Daniel slept little by choice, feeling at peace with his surroundings. Memories of a challenging rite of passage in his youth, when he was sent into the wilderness to survive alone for ten weeks, filled him with reflections on growth and possibility.

Above, the dawn painted the sky with breathtaking hues, heralding a new day as creatures stirred, ready to embrace it.

As he prepared to return to Paris, Daniel reflected on the harmony and balance he had rediscovered during his time in Africa, feeling ready to re-engage with the urban pace. After settling into his new home, he strolled the city's iconic streets, visited renowned landmarks, including the spiritually resonant Notre Dame, which deepened his connection to history. This journey reaffirmed for Daniel the importance of spirituality in leading a balanced life. His African experiences ignited a quest for wisdom, underscoring the need for harmony with nature and attentiveness to its subtle cues.

He frequented local food markets and experimented with the recipes he'd discovered in Africa. Thoughtfully, he began journaling and drafted a list of aspirations and areas he wished to release from his life. This process clarified his intentions, preparing him to turn his newfound dreams into reality. He realized he no longer desired career accolades, long hours, hectic schedules, or the stress that accompanied them. Instead, he aspired to create something meaningful and unique, embodying his vision of a balanced life centered on purpose, delivering real value to others, focusing on health and wellness, and giving back to the community.

As his thoughts spun and clarified, he envisioned a unique upscale community center in the St. Germain des Pres arrondissement in Paris, an expansive space tucked away behind a group of historical buildings flanking one of the infamous narrow cobbled streets. Studios would be available for health-related classes, including meditation, yoga, Pilates, gym workouts, and classical and modern dance, while the juice and health food bar would attract an eclectic clientele. The building would be completely solar-powered, and an upscale restaurant would offer cuisine inspired by chefs from Botswana. The organic menu would feature authentic fare from their homeland, fused with homegrown produce from local Parisian family farms and herbs grown in the building's expansive rooftop garden, freshly picked daily. The head chef would host weekly classes for the community and surprise pop-up events with eco-chefs and wellness enthusiasts invited from around the world.

Interestingly, Daniel's concepts aligned perfectly with Paris's plans to become the most eco-friendly city in Europe, making the timing exceptionally opportune.[12] The interior space would evolve into an architectural marvel while the exterior would preserve the traditional charm of the neighborhood. The ambiance inside would reflect the inspirations Daniel drew from his trip to Africa, and he planned to collaborate with an architect from Botswana to bring this vision to life. The space would feature handcrafted pieces made by skilled artisans from Botswana, with these unique items available for purchase on the website. A percentage of all profits from the businesses would support local craftsmen, architects, and artists in Botswana, as well as the Peace Corps LIFE project with which he had previously been involved.

Yearly draws for an all-expenses-paid family safari would incentivize his new clientele and help educate a broader audience about the work being done, the environmental issues at stake, and the need to prevent large businesses from disrupting the crucial eco-balance the retreats aimed to maintain.

Initially, Daniel would oversee these projects, attracting an excellent team to take the lead over time, allowing him to settle into a simpler, minimalistic life with opportunities to return to South Africa and visit old friends. As he envisioned these possibilities, he felt deeply attuned to their purpose, and a profound sense of gratitude washed over him.

Daniel's story reveals that meditation doesn't have to be rigid; it can involve quiet time in nature, a walking ritual, or simply pausing to breathe. It's about finding presence in the moment and creating mental space to reconnect with oneself.

Case Study:

Jonathan, Professor at The American University in Cairo, Egypt - Meditation Journey

In the vibrant city of Cairo, Egypt, Dr. Jonathan Blake—a respected professor of Middle Eastern Studies at the American University—was drawn to meditation, not only as part of his research but also to balance his intellectual pursuits with the demands of modern life. Immersed in the rich historical tapestry of the region, Dr. Blake's work involved extensive research, lectures, and often grueling administrative responsibilities, which gradually took a toll on his mental clarity and sense of peace.

Discovering Meditation

Dr. Blake's introduction to meditation occurred during a faculty retreat focused on stress management and professional development. He was captivated by the potential of meditation to foster tranquility and focus, mirroring the philosophical teachings of ancient cultures he admired. This alignment with historical mindfulness sparked his curiosity to explore meditation techniques as a major part of his research.

Embracing Techniques for Modern Living

Back in Cairo, Dr. Blake integrated meditation into his daily routine, complementing his academic life. Each morning, he devoted time to focus-led meditation sessions in his study overlooking the city. This calming practice provided him with resilience, allowing him to approach his work with renewed vigor.

Throughout the day, amidst lectures and research discussions, Dr. Blake utilized short meditation intervals to recalibrate his focus. These sessions enhanced his cognitive abilities and offered creative solutions to academic challenges, teaching him the necessary balance to effectively manage academic pressures.

Navigating the Path

While implementing meditation as a transformative practice, Dr. Blake faced obstacles. Initially, he struggled to maintain consistency amidst rigorous schedules and the fast pace of city life. However, this struggle underscored the importance of perseverance, deepening his resolve on the mindfulness journey.

Transformative Impact

Dr. Blake's meditation practice led to both personal and professional transformations. His newfound tranquility was contagious; students and colleagues noted his enhanced clarity and empathy. This inspired others within the university to explore similar practices, prompting Dr. Blake to organize meditation workshops and travel retreats that highlighted its benefits for academic growth.

Dr. Blake's journey exemplifies the potent synergy between ancient meditation practices and modern living, showcasing mindfulness's role in enhancing life quality. His story invites others to consider integrating meditation into their daily routines, offering a compelling narrative about personal and community evolution through dedicated, mindful practice.

Like Daniel and Dr. Blake, people throughout history have turned to meditation to find clarity and meaning. From sacred mountains to royal courts, ancient cultures developed rich traditions that continue to shape modern meditation practices.

Meditation Across Ancient Cultures: Historical Insight

Hindu Tradition: The Timeless Practice of Dharana

In the lush landscapes of ancient India, meditation was more than a practice; it was a way of life, intricately woven into the fabric of Hindu tradition. Known as "dharana," this form of meditation centered on concentration and was considered a preliminary stage to deeper meditation, or "dhyana." Sages and yogis would retreat into serene ashrams, often nestled within sacred groves, to cultivate mental calmness and spiritual enlightenment.

The Hindu scriptures, particularly the Upanishads, emphasize meditation as a path to attaining moksha, or liberation from the cycle of rebirth. By focusing on a single point or deity, practitioners learned to control their minds and transcend the material world, seeking unity with the divine.

Legend tells of the sage Patanjali, revered as the father of yoga, who composed the "Yoga Sutras," a foundational text outlining the philosophy and practice of yoga and meditation. Through structured practices, individuals were guided to achieve stillness and insight, reflecting the innate harmony of the universe.

Daoist Tradition: Harmony with the Tao

Meanwhile, in ancient China, Daoist masters shared a similar reverence for meditation, believing it essential for harmonizing the body, mind, and spirit with the Tao—the fundamental nature of the world. Meditation in Daoism focused on inner stillness and cultivating "qi," or life energy, to align oneself with cosmic forces, maintaining health and spiritual attainment.

Practitioners often secluded themselves in mountainous regions, believed to be rich with spiritual energy. Here, techniques such as "zuo wang" or "sitting and forgetting" were developed, requiring the release of worldly concerns and identities to align with the Dao and achieve tranquility and insight.

Ancient Daoist texts, like the "Tao Te Ching" attributed to Laozi, underscored the importance of living in accordance with nature, viewing meditation as a natural expression of this philosophy.

Buddhist Tradition: The Middle Path of Mindfulness

Buddhist meditation, a cornerstone of the spiritual practice founded by Siddhartha Gautama, or the Buddha, focuses on achieving mindful awareness and enlightenment.[13] Central to Buddhism is understanding the mind and eliminating suffering through practices like mindfulness (Sati), concentration (Samadhi), and insight (Vipassana). These practices cultivate present-moment awareness, allowing practitioners to perceive reality's true nature.

Rooted in Buddhist texts and teachings, meditation practices such as Anapanasati (mindfulness of breathing) and Metta Bhavana (loving-kindness meditation) offer pathways to develop compassion, patience, and spiritual insight. Over centuries, these practices have been adapted and adopted globally, influencing both secular and spiritual meditation techniques in modern wellness. They are viewed not only as a means to spiritual awakening but also as tools for fostering mental clarity and emotional well-being in everyday life. This universal appeal underscores the timeless and transformative potential of Buddhist meditation principles across cultures and epochs.

Egyptian Tradition: Aligning With the Cosmos

In the storied land of ancient Egypt (originally known as "Kemet"), meditation was deeply woven into spirituality and cosmology. At its core, Kemet was a land of sages, mystics, and scholars who discerned a deeper reality beyond the physical world. The Egyptians believed in the harmony of body, mind, and spirit, with meditation playing a crucial role. Central to their practice was "Ma'at," the principle of truth, balance, and cosmic order, reflected in the daily lives and spiritual practices of the people.[14]

Kemetic Deities

Gods and goddesses played essential roles in the universe, serving as accessible entities within the cosmos, providing wisdom and inspiration. Notable deities included:[15]

- **Ra (or Re)**: The Sun God, symbolizing creation, rebirth, and the cyclical nature of life.
- **Isis**: Goddess of healing, magic, and motherhood, offering protection and insight to her followers.
- **Anubis**: Guardian of the afterlife, guiding souls and ensuring their safe passage into the next realm.
- **Osiris**: Symbolizing resurrection and the afterlife, Osiris offers insights into life's cyclical nature and the eternal journey of the soul.
- **Hathor**: The goddess of love, beauty, and music, Hathor harnesses the healing power of music and dance.
- **Thoth**: The god of wisdom, writing, and magic, Thoth fosters clearer insights, deeper understanding, and a stronger connection to ancient wisdom.

Kemetic Meditation

Meditation was intricately woven into the daily rituals that marked the rhythm of life. Mornings often began with offerings to the deities, accompanied by meditative chants as the sun rose. Throughout the day, practitioners utilized various forms of meditation—ranging from silent contemplation to dance and song—to maintain harmony with the universe.

Priests and priestesses engaged in meditative practices to connect with the divine, employing visualization techniques with symbols like the "Eye of Horus" and "Ankh" to achieve enlightenment. They used sacred oils, incense, and specific postures to reach deeper states of consciousness, allowing them to journey to astral realms or communicate with the gods.

Enhancements Through Scent and Sound

Fragrances elevated relaxation and spiritual awareness, serving as offerings to the deities. Sound elements enriched the meditative experience, guiding practitioners to deeper states of consciousness.

Traditional Scents:

- **Frankincense**: Commonly used in ancient Kemet, it promotes tranquility and enhances spiritual awareness.
- **Myrrh**: Esteemed for purifying spaces and welcoming protective energies.

- **Lotus**: A sacred scent in ancient Egypt, it inspires clarity, spiritual awakening, and enlightenment.

Sound Vibrations:

- **Ancient Kemetic Hymns**: Sacred hymns and chants invoke spiritual resonance, immersing practitioners in ethereal vibrations.
- **Sistrum**: A traditional musical instrument from ancient Egypt, its soothing resonance can slow the heart rate and support entry into a calm, introspective state.
- **Nature Sounds**: When meditating outdoors, embrace natural sounds like birdsong, the rustling of leaves, and flowing water to guide your meditation journey.

Key Elements of Egyptian Meditation

- **Inner Light Visualization**: Spend 10–20 minutes with your eyes closed, taking slow, deep breaths. Visualize a cleansing light filling your body from head to toe, purging negative energy and replacing it with positivity.
- **Breath of the Gods**: In a quiet setting, sit comfortably and close your eyes. Inhale deeply to a count of four, hold for four, then exhale for four. As you repeat this cycle, visualize energy circulating through your body, connecting you to ancient wisdom.

- **The Heart-Feather Meditation (Ma'at's Balance)**: Seated with your eyes closed, focus on your heart. Visualize a feather resting there, symbolizing lightness, balance, and truth. Contemplate heavy emotions or thoughts, imagining them dissolving into light, bringing peace and equilibrium.

- **Sacred Geometry Focus (The Ankh Meditation)**: Sit comfortably with closed eyes. Visualize the ankh symbol radiating light. Feel its energy entering your body, revitalizing and harmonizing each cell as you breathe deeply.

- **Sound Chanting with Egyptian Words of Power and Temple of the Mind Visualization**: In a comfortable position with eyes closed, focus on your breath. Choose a power word like "Ra" (the ancient Egyptian sun god, invoking feelings of illumination and vitality) and chant it softly, allowing the vibrations to resonate throughout your body. Visualize these vibrations clearing negative blocks and opening channels to higher consciousness. Continue for several minutes.

These techniques provide enhanced clarity, stress relief, and a deeper spiritual connection, inviting practitioners to engage with the rich mystical traditions of ancient Egypt.

Exploring Egyptian meditation techniques can infuse your life with mysticism and spiritual insight. By immersing yourself in these methods, you'll discover tranquility and a connection to one of humanity's oldest spiritual traditions.

African Tradition: Harmony Among the Individual, Community, and Environment

Across various regions of the African continent, meditation has long been a foundational practice tied to spirituality, community, and healing. African meditation practices are deeply intertwined with the rich tapestry of spiritual traditions throughout the continent. Rooted in oral traditions and ancestral teachings, these practices emphasize the integral role of community and nature in achieving mental and spiritual balance.

African meditation often highlights the unity between the individual and the collective, reflecting a holistic understanding of health that encompasses mind, body, and spirit. This interconnectedness is echoed in rituals and communal gatherings, typically led by spiritual leaders or healers who guide participants in shared meditative and contemplative practices. Many of these methods aim to connect individuals with their ancestors and the natural world, fostering grounding and inner peace.

A distinctive feature of African meditation is its incorporation of music and dance, which serve as meditative tools for spiritual awakening and emotional expression. Rhythmic drumming and chanting often accompany meditation gatherings, creating an immersive experience that fosters trance states and deeper spiritual insights.

As modern society embraces holistic healing, African meditation offers timeless wisdom—rooted in nature, community, and spiritual balance—that continues to inspire contemporary wellness practices.

Shamanic Tradition: Nature, Rituals, and Vision Quests

Shamanic meditation, one of the world's oldest spiritual practices, originated in ancient cultures across Siberia, Mongolia, and the Americas, emphasizing a deep connection with nature and the spirit realm.

Shamanism often involves entering altered states of consciousness to interact with the spirit world and gain insights for healing and guidance. This practice is deeply rooted in indigenous traditions, which utilize rituals, drumming, and chanting to facilitate these journeys.

Shamans, the practitioners of this form of meditation, act as mediators between the physical and spiritual realms. Through meditation, they embark on spiritual quests or journeys, often described as traveling across realms to seek wisdom or healing. Each experience is deeply personal, uniquely tailored to the shaman's intentions and community needs.

Central to shamanic meditation is the belief in the interconnectedness of all life, a concept shared by many shamanic cultures, from Siberian indigenous groups to Native American tribes. These practices guide individuals to connect deeply with nature, spirits, and their subconscious, promoting holistic healing and personal growth.

In modern applications, shamanic meditation is gaining popularity as a tool for exploring consciousness and fostering spiritual development. As more people seek non-traditional forms of healing and self-discovery, shamanic practices offer valuable insights into ancient meditation methods that align with the quest for balance and wholeness in contemporary life. The integration of these age-old techniques into modern wellness regimes underscores the timeless relevance of shamanic meditation practices in achieving spiritual coherence and harmony.

Comparing and Contrasting Global Meditation Practices

To highlight the common threads across traditions, here's a comparison of meditation styles from around the world.

Tradition	Origin	Focus/Practice	Common Elements	Unique Aspects
Buddhism	India	Mindfulness, meditation on impermanence	Mindfulness, insight, meditation	Emphasizes inner peace and wisdom
Hinduism	India	Dharana (concentration)	Concentration, liberation (moksha)	Focused on spiritual liberation
Taoism	China	Harmony with Tao, inner stillness	Meditative stillness, qi cultivation	Aligning with cosmic forces

African Meditation

- Connection to nature and ancestral spirits
- Community rituals, rhythm, and nature
- Rooted in traditional cultural practices

Christian Contemplative Prayer

- Christian tradition
- Experiencing God's presence
- Prayer, silence, and scripture reflection
- Deep personal communion with God

Jain Meditation

- Internal journeys and spiritual discipline
- Ascetic practices and non-violence
- Spiritual purity for liberation

Japa Meditation

- Hindu tradition
- Repeating mantras or deity names
- Chanting, repetition, and concentration
- Enhancing spiritual growth through mantra

Kabbalistic Meditation

- Jewish tradition
- Exploring the inner dimensions of the Torah
- Mysticism and divine connection
- Focus on hidden spiritual realities

Native American Vision Quest

- Native American practices
- Meditation and fasting for spiritual guidance
- Insight through solitude in nature

Qigong

- Chinese practice
- Breath alignment, movement, and awareness
- Integrates health practices with meditation

Shamanic Meditation

- Global indigenous practices

- Journeying and altered states of consciousness
- Rituals, drumming, and spirits
- Interacting with spiritual realms

Sufi Meditation

- Islamic region focus
- Divine love and heart-centered practices
- Devotional activities and chanting
- Mystical connection to God

Transcendental Meditation

- Indian roots
- Silent mantra meditation
- Mantras for relaxation and stress relief
- Simplified practice for stress reduction

Vipassana Meditation

- Indian tradition
- Cultivating insight through silence
- Observing sensations and reality

Zen Meditation

- Japanese origins
- Insight into the nature of mind and reality
- Self-restraint and zazen (seated meditation)
- Awareness of non-duality

Despite their differences, these practices all share a commitment to cultivating presence, peace, and spiritual growth—universal goals for our modern lives.

Meditation Today: Techniques for Modern Living

Meditation techniques today draw deeply from ancient concepts, integrating wisdom from diverse cultures worldwide. Traditional methods, such as mindfulness with roots in Buddhist practices, emphasize a strong connection between breath and the present moment. Modern adaptations have expanded this to include mindful walking, which embraces movement alongside mental focus. Additionally, Transcendental Meditation (TM), derived from Indian traditions, fosters tranquility through the silent repetition of mantras. Zen meditation, or Zazen, emphasizes posture and attentiveness, reflecting its Japanese origins. In today's fast-paced society, these ancient techniques have evolved into accessible practices, adapted to suit various lifestyles and psychological needs, underscoring a global, time-honored quest for inner peace and clarity.

Mindfulness Meditation - Originating from Buddhist practices, this technique focuses on the present moment without judgment and is widely used to enhance mindfulness and reduce stress.

Transcendental Meditation - A technique rooted in Vedic traditions, TM involves silently reciting a mantra, promoting deep relaxation and heightened alertness. It has been featured in various literary and media contexts, with notable advocates such as David Lynch, Paul McCartney and Oprah Winfrey. Debates surrounding TM often focus on its effectiveness and scientific credibility. While some praise its benefits, critics call for more rigorous studies. Nevertheless, many schools have incorporated TM into their curricula due to its recognized benefits in stress reduction and enhanced cognitive function.[17,18]

Guided Visualization - This technique involves forming mental images of relaxing places or situations with the help of a guide or instructor, making it ideal for relaxation and stress management.

Zen Meditation (Zazen) - Part of Zen Buddhism, Zazen is a seated meditation that emphasizes observing thoughts and surroundings without attachment. Steve Jobs's practice of Zazen illustrates meditation's tangible impact on creativity, leadership, and personal growth. After an intuitive need to visit India at age 19, studying under Zen Master Kobun Chino Otogawa, he adopted six principles that guided his life and work:

- **Your Mess Is Your Medicine:** Turn failures into opportunities for growth, building resilience through adversity.

- **The Future Belongs to Conscious Leaders:** Practice awareness and mindfulness in leadership to drive positive change.
- **Structure Enhances Your Spirit:** Establish routines and systems that support creativity and maintain balance.
- **Your Sensitivity Is a Strength, Not a Weakness:** Cultivate empathy and insight as sources of creativity and leadership.
- **Less Is More:** Champion simplicity in design and thought, a hallmark of Apple's innovation.
- **Fill Your Life With Great Work:** Pursue purpose-driven projects that challenge and fulfill, aligning with your values.

These insights, paired with teachings from "Be Here Now" by Ram Dass, illuminated Steve Jobs's personal and professional transformation, reshaping his life's mission.[19]

He infused mindful awareness and simplicity into his daily life, closely aligning with the meditative path of focusing on what truly matters.

Focused Meditation - This technique utilizes concentration on something internal or external (like breathing or a candle flame) to enhance focus.

Loving-kindness Meditation (Metta) - This practice aims to increase compassion and kindness by mentally sending goodwill and kind thoughts to oneself and others.

- **Breath Awareness and Body Scan** - Both techniques encourage inward attention—either to the breath or body—helping relieve stress, improve emotional clarity, and ground the practitioner.
- **Movement Meditation** - Incorporating mindfulness into movement, such as yoga, tai chi, or walking, promotes physical wellness alongside mental clarity.
- **Chakra Meditation** - This technique focuses on balancing the energy centers of the body, often used for spiritual growth and physical prosperity.

Review and Implement

Define Your Intentions - Fuel Your Progress

Quick Checklist

To deepen your meditation journey, practice with clear goals and intentional focus. Select techniques that match your experience level, remain aware of common challenges unique to each stage, and employ practical troubleshooting strategies to maintain momentum. This targeted approach helps reinforce consistency and encourages reflection for continuous improvement. Here's a detailed guide:

Beginner Level: Guided Meditation

- **What's New:** Embrace structured guidance—through apps, recordings, or live sessions—to establish routine and build foundational skills.

- **Key Technique**: Mindful Breathing—anchor attention through the breath, using guidance to refocus when mind-wandering occurs.
- **Reinforcement**: When discomfort, distractions, or restlessness arise (e.g., during body scans), calmly adjust your position and remember that ease develops over time.
- **How to integrate:** Incorporate a short recorded or live session into your morning or bedtime routines. Use guided tracks during work breaks or after stressful moments. Practice mindful breathing while waiting in line or before meals.

Intermediate Level: Mindfulness Meditation

- **What's New**: Begin integrating practice into daily activities—such as mindful walking or basic Metta (loving-kindness).
- **Key Technique**: Expand your focus from breath to sensations, thoughts, and emotions, all observed without judgment.
- **Reinforcement**: If distracted, slow your experience, concentrating on the immediacy of your movement (if walking), or start with someone easy to love in Metta before extending compassion.
- **How to integrate:** Weave mindfulness into everyday tasks—while walking, eating, or commuting.

Set reminders for "awareness check-ins" throughout the day. Use brief bursts of loving-kindness or walking meditation when transitioning between tasks.

Advanced Level: Silent/Mantra-Based Meditation

- **What's New:** Explore advanced styles such as Transcendental Meditation (TM), Vipassana, or Zazen—requiring sustained silence or focus on a mantra.

- **Key Technique**: Utilize repetitive sounds or deep insight meditations to access profound states of calm and clarity.

- **Reinforcement**: Recognize that slow progress is part of the journey—patience is essential. Minor discomfort or frustration can be reframed as motivation for present-moment focus.

- **How to integrate:** Dedicate a consistent time and quiet space—early morning or evening often works best. Establish a personal ritual (light a candle, set a timer, journal after sessions) to reinforce commitment. When time is tight, re-center with a few silent breaths or mantra repetitions.

As we transition from our exploration of mindfulness and meditation, we open the door to understanding how natural healing methods beautifully complement these practices. While meditation offers a journey inward, helping us find calm and clarity, natural healing methods nourish the body and mind from the outside. These healing modalities tap into the wisdom of the earth, providing remedies and treatments that align with the principles of balance and well-being inherent in meditation. Get ready to weave natural healing into the very fabric of your everyday experience.

CHAPTER 4

EMBRACING NATURAL HEALING

Case Study:

Emma, Artist in Paris, France - Ayurvedic Journey Offers Relief from Chronic Health Issues

Emma, a passionate artist living in the bustling heart of Paris, struggled with chronic discomfort and fatigue for several years. Despite numerous visits to conventional doctors, she found herself trapped in a cycle of temporary relief and recurring symptoms. Her journey took a transformative turn when she decided to explore Ayurveda—a centuries-old system of natural healing rooted in Indian tradition.

Intrigued by Ayurveda's holistic approach, which emphasizes balancing body, mind, and spirit through natural means, Emma embarked on a quest for recovery. She consulted a renowned Ayurvedic practitioner, who conducted a thorough assessment of her lifestyle, diet, and mental state.

Understanding the Doshas

The practitioner introduced Emma to the concept of Doshas—Vata, Pitta, and Kapha—unique combinations of physical, emotional, and mental characteristics that influence individual health. Emma discovered that many of her symptoms stemmed from a Vata imbalance, exacerbated by irregular routines, stress, and poor eating habits.

Embracing Ayurvedic Practices

Emma committed to a personalized Ayurvedic regimen designed to restore balance to her Doshas. This included incorporating a diet rich in warm, nourishing foods and herbs like turmeric and ginger, known for their anti-inflammatory and healing properties. She added daily oil massages (Abhyanga) and calming yoga flows to help quiet her mind and ground her energy.

Her practitioner also guided her toward mindfulness and meditation to cultivate a serene mental state, a crucial component of Ayurvedic healing. These practices helped Emma attune to her body's needs, reducing stress and enhancing her overall sense of well-being.

Transformation and Holistic Wellness

Over the following months, Emma experienced a significant transformation. The symptoms that once dominated her daily life began to subside, replaced by renewed vitality and creativity. Her sleep improved, anxiety diminished, and she became more attuned to her body's rhythms.

Emma's experience with Ayurveda reveals how ancient practices can offer sustainable wellness—not just in healing the body, but in creating daily rhythms that support long-term vitality.

Case Study:

Mei, Educator in Guangdong - Healing through the Wisdom of Traditional Chinese Medicine

In the rolling hills of rural Guangdong, Mei, a young woman burdened by chronic migraines and fatigue, sought refuge in Traditional Chinese Medicine (TCM). Her conventional medical treatments had offered little relief, prompting her to explore these ancient practices acclaimed for balancing body energy and fostering health.

In addition to her journey toward wellness through TCM, Mei is a dedicated art teacher at a local community center, where she merges creativity with emotional expression. Her career involves not just instructing students in painting and sculpture techniques, but also in utilizing art as a therapeutic medium for personal healing.

Mei's natural flair for teaching and deep appreciation for aesthetic beauty have earned her a cherished place among her students. To Mei, both TCM and art promote harmony by aligning emotion, intention, and energy—a reflection of her belief that healing is as much creative as it is clinical. This dual approach has made her classes popular, offering a sanctuary for individuals seeking both artistic skill and emotional respite.

Her classroom is a vibrant amalgamation of colors, inspirations, and calm—a reflection of her philosophy that art and healing walk hand in hand, nurturing the soul and inspiring growth. Mei's professional life demonstrates that traditional healing wisdom, alongside modern creativity, provides a path for her students to achieve harmony in their lives.

Mei's journey began with a visit to a renowned TCM practitioner in her hometown. The doctor, skilled in modalities passed down through generations, conducted a thorough examination, considering not just her symptoms but her lifestyle, diet, and emotional state. Unlike the segmented approach she had experienced before, this was a comprehensive evaluation aimed at understanding her unique energetic makeup.

Diagnosis and Treatment: Balancing the Qi

Mei's diagnosis indicated an imbalance in her Qi—the vital life force per TCM—caused by stress and lifestyle choices that disrupted her body's natural harmony. To restore equilibrium, the practitioner prescribed a series of treatments encompassing acupuncture, herbal medicine, and dietary adjustments rooted in TCM philosophy.

The acupuncture sessions were particularly transformative. Mei found relief as fine needles were meticulously placed to stimulate her body's meridians, targeting pressure points corresponding to her headaches and fatigue. Each session left her with a palpable sense of relief and calm she hadn't previously experienced.

Complementing her acupuncture, Mei adopted a custom herbal tea regimen—ginseng to boost energy and peony root to calm her mind—becoming a welcome part of her daily routine.

Integrating Lifestyle Changes

Beyond treatments, Mei adjusted her lifestyle, adopting TCM-informed practices to bolster her recovery. She learned the importance of living in harmony with the seasons, making diet and activity choices that shifted with the time of year—like eating warm, hearty foods in winter and lighter, cooling meals in summer.

Moreover, a focus on mindfulness and meditation enhanced her emotional well-being, aligning her more deeply with both her body and spirit. Mei adopted gentle exercises similar to Qigong, integrating physical movement, breathing, and meditative focus to reinforce her internal balance.

Rejuvenation and Reflection

Over time, Mei's symptoms receded, replaced by newfound vitality and inner peace. Her commitment to TCM principles transformed not just her health but also her outlook on life, making balance a way of living rather than merely a treatment outcome. Mei's journey underscores the rich benefits of a holistic approach, blending ancient practices with mindful living.

Her rejuvenation not only alleviated the burdens of her physical ailments but also revealed a life philosophy that provided deeper, lasting well-being—an essence that many contemporary practices aspire to capture.

Natural Remedies and Their Benefits: A Comparison Table

The comparison table below provides an overview of several natural remedies and their benefits. Each remedy has unique strengths that support various aspects of physical and emotional well-being, showcasing the diverse potential of natural healing approaches.

It is essential to maintain open communication with your doctor, especially when taking medications, to avoid any adverse interactions, particularly when introducing new elements into your regimen. For example, certain foods like grapefruit can interfere with the effectiveness of drugs used to lower cholesterol or treat high blood pressure.[1] Additionally, reviewing resources on interactions between herbal products and medications is important.[2]

Like Emma and Mei, many individuals are turning to natural remedies as a supplement to conventional care. The following comparison chart introduces several popular natural healing agents and their core benefits, offering a starting point for your exploration.

Natural Remedy	Benefits
Aloe Vera	Soothes skin irritations and promotes healing when applied topically; supports digestive health internally.
Ashwagandha	Adaptogen that helps the body manage stress; enhances mood, memory, and physical endurance.
Chamomile	Promotes relaxation and improves sleep quality; helps with anxiety and digestive issues.

Cinnamon	Contains antioxidants and has anti-inflammatory properties; supports blood sugar regulation and heart health.
Cranberry	Prevents urinary tract infections by inhibiting bacterial adhesion to the bladder wall; rich in antioxidants.
Echinacea	Supports the immune system and may reduce the duration of colds and upper respiratory infections.
Fenugreek	Aids digestion and helps regulate blood sugar levels; supports lactation in breastfeeding mothers.
Garlic	Supports cardiovascular health by reducing blood pressure and cholesterol levels; has anti-microbial properties that aid the immune system.
Ginger	Anti-inflammatory and aids digestion; reduces nausea and soothes sore muscles.
Ginkgo Biloba	Improves memory and cognitive function; supports circulation and brain health.
Ginseng	Boosts energy, enhances physical performance, and improves mental clarity; supports the immune system.
Holy Basil (Tulsi)	Helps reduce stress and anxiety; supports immune function and has anti-inflammatory properties.

Lavender	Calms and reduces anxiety; aids restful sleep and is used in aromatherapy for stress relief.
Milk Thistle	Supports liver health by improving detoxification and reducing liver inflammation.
Peppermint	Relieves digestive issues such as IBS; alleviates headaches and muscle pain.
Rosemary	Enhances memory and concentration; has anti-inflammatory properties and aids digestion.
St. John's Wort	Commonly used to treat mild to moderate depression and anxiety; supports emotional balance.
Tea Tree Oil	Antimicrobial properties make it effective in treating skin infections and acne; used in various topical applications.
Turmeric	Contains curcumin, which offers anti-inflammatory and antioxidant effects; supports joint health and reduces inflammation.
Valerian Root	Natural sleep aid that may improve sleep quality and reduce symptoms of insomnia.

Important: While these remedies offer many benefits, always consult a healthcare provider, especially if you have existing conditions or take medication. Natural remedies can be powerful, and it's crucial to ensure they are appropriate for your health profile.

Align Your Strategy - Propel Your Progress

Quick Checklist

Beginner-Friendly Guide to Natural Healing

1. Practical Tips for Beginners

Start Small: Introduce one remedy at a time and use it consistently for at least 1–2 weeks before adding another, allowing you to observe its effects clearly.

Keep Records: Document your experiences and any reactions.

Mind Quality: Use high-quality, organic products whenever possible.

2. Identify Well-Researched and Effective Remedies

Use trusted sources to guide your initial steps.

3. Vetting Alternative Medicine Practices

Research Practitioner Credentials: Check for reputable certifications, professional affiliations, and endorsements by health authorities.

Look for Scientific Evidence: Seek evidence-based studies and clinical trials supporting the remedies.

4. Precautions and Awareness

Allergies and Interactions: Be mindful of potential allergies and interactions with current medications.

An Open Mind: Combine natural methods with conventional medicine sensibly.

Listen to Your Body: Pay attention to your body's responses and adjust as needed.

5. Consult with Healthcare Professionals

Consultation: Seek advice from certified naturopaths or doctors trained in both conventional and alternative medicine approaches.

6. Verify Product Labels

Ingredients: Check for certifications and ingredient lists to ensure reliability.

Herbal Medicine: Involves using plant extracts for medicinal purposes.

7. Conduct Patch Tests

Test remedies like essential oils on a small area of skin to check for allergies.

8. Maintain a Log

Record remedies used and any effects or side effects.

9. Some Common Natural Remedies

Body-Based Therapies

Acupuncture: Involves inserting thin needles into specific points on the body to relieve pain, reduce stress, and manage various health conditions based on traditional Chinese medicine.

Auriculotherapy: Applies pressure or uses needles on the ear, an area believed to correspond with different health conditions, to address issues such as pain and stress.

Bioidentical Dentistry: A progressive field focusing on biologically compatible materials aligned with the body's natural functions. This approach enhances oral health by using materials that mimic natural tooth composition, promoting healing and reducing allergic reactions and toxicity found in traditional materials.

Chiropractic Care: Focuses on diagnosing and treating musculoskeletal disorders, particularly through spine adjustments to alleviate pain and improve mobility.

Cupping Therapy: Involves placing cups on the skin to create suction, believed to improve blood flow, reduce muscle tension, and promote healing.

Hydrotherapy: Employs water in various forms (hot/cold baths, steam) to alleviate discomfort like muscle pain and arthritis while promoting circulation.

Reflexology: Applies pressure to specific points on the feet, hands, or ears that correspond to various organs, promoting relaxation and health.

Yoga: Combines physical postures, breathing exercises, and meditation to enhance flexibility, mental focus, and spiritual alignment.

Energy Healing & Mind-Body

Ayurveda: An ancient holistic system from India that emphasizes balancing bodily systems through diet, herbal treatments, and holistic practices such as yoga.

Homeopathy: Employs highly diluted substances to stimulate the body's natural healing processes, based on the principle of "like cures like."

Hypnotherapy: Utilizes guided relaxation and focused attention to achieve a heightened state of consciousness, fostering behavior change and emotional release.

Reiki: An energy healing practice in which practitioners direct the flow of energy within the body to promote balance and well-being.

Sensory-Based Practices

Aromatherapy: Harnesses essential oils to elevate mood, ease tension, and create a calming environment conducive to restful sleep.

Music Therapy: Leverages the power of vibrations and sound frequencies measured in Hertz (Hz) to promote healing and enhance well-being. By using specific tones and melodies, music therapy aligns with the body's natural frequencies, facilitating relaxation and emotional release.

Sound Bathing: Envelops the body in continuous healing vibrations from instruments like singing bowls and gongs, gently guiding the mind toward meditative clarity and emotional release.

Ingestible or Supplement-Based

Herbal Medicine: Utilizes plant extracts for medicinal purposes, addressing conditions such as inflammation and supporting the immune system.

Nutritional Supplements: Offers dietary support with vitamins, minerals, and other nutrients to fill dietary gaps and promote overall health.

These remedies provide diverse approaches to natural health and wellness, often complementing conventional medical treatments to enhance quality of life and alleviate various health challenges.

As we carry these natural healing principles forward, we will explore how to create balance among work, life, and self-care—discovering how mindful choices can help you build a more harmonious daily rhythm.

CHAPTER 5

ACHIEVING WORK-LIFE BALANCE

Case Study:

Esme, Farming and Gastronomy in the Basque Country - Addressing Chronic Health Issues

Founded in 1203, the charming Basque town of Hondarribia features medieval architecture and walls that testify to centuries of strategic importance and community resilience.[1,2] Beneath these ramparts, the Laxta sheep unique to the region graze on fertile hills, their rich milk producing the celebrated Idiazábal cheese.[3,4] Down by the water's edge, the narrow cobblestone streets of San Pedro, Santiago, and Santa María echo with the legacy of the Cofradía de Mareantes (Fisherman's Brotherhood) of San Pedro, established in 1361, whose maritime bounty continues to shape local gastronomy.[5]

The town's ancient roots run deeper than its stonework: Euskara, a pre-Indo-European language isolate dating back over 12,000 years, endures in everyday speech.[6] In 2021, researchers uncovered the Hand of Irulegi—a 2,100-year-old inscription bearing two words similar to modern Euskara—suggesting that Pamplona, renowned for its San Fermin Festival and running of the bulls, may indeed be the cradle of the Basque people, a mystery that has long baffled historians. Art offers other clues, including the 40,000-year-old cave paintings in Danbolinzulo Cave near Zestoa in Spain, linking present-day residents to their prehistoric ancestors. Against this tapestry of prehistoric art, ancestral tongue, and intergenerational culinary craft—where humble, locally sourced ingredients yield dishes renowned worldwide—Hondarribia offers a timeless taste of Basque identity and tradition.[7,8,9]

It was within this rich backdrop that Esme grew up on her family's sheep farm, surrounded by lush greenery. At dawn, she led the sheep across dew-kissed grasses, learning the rhythms of pastoral life and the deep connections among land, sea, community, and sustenance. These formative years instilled in her a respect for tradition, the seasons, and the resilient spirit of her Basque heritage.

In recent years, Esme's family opened a restaurant on the bustling marina, nestled among Hondarribia's quaint fishermen's houses. While San Sebastian is often hailed as the Basque culinary capital, Hondarribia's laid-back charm and traditional ambiance provide a welcome alternative, attracting global tourists and locals eager to savor fresh, local delights.[10]

Her interactions with visitors, including a South Florida chef named Niven, sparked an opportunity to collaborate on a fusion-inspired venture on the Miami waterfront that would blend Basque culinary traditions with global influences such as Japanese and Latin.

Relocating to the vibrant, culturally rich city of Miami brought Esme excitement and growth, yet she faced challenges adapting to the rapid pace, leading to stress-related health issues. Long hours, lack of sleep, and reliance on fast food took a toll. Often, she longed to be back with her woolly sheep in the hills of her family farm, enjoying nature and conversing with locals by the marina in Hondarribia. Occasionally, she would fly home for a weekend, seeking mental space, quality time with relatives, and a chance to recharge.

Inspired by Miami's growing organic movement, Esme became passionate about promoting clean, sustainable eating—both in her own life and in her restaurant's mission. Recognizing the global impact of chronic health issues and the movement toward healthier living, she educated herself on functional and holistic health modalities, seeking answers for her own autoimmune and thyroid issues, early signs of rheumatoid arthritis, and related concerns. She shared her ideas with Niven, explaining how the Miami restaurant could play a vital role in helping others facing similar struggles. They transformed part of the space into a community hub promoting organic foods and sustainable practices. The rooftop was converted into a garden for growing fresh vegetables and herbs for the restaurant, accompanied by a tavern where patrons could enjoy food and drinks in a relaxed atmosphere, savoring the fresh sea breezes.

Esme worked directly with private clients eager to embrace healthier choices. She guided them on private tours through local grocery stores and fresh markets, emphasizing the importance of reading labels, understanding ingredients, and focusing on fresh, organic produce. She visited their homes to help create healthier kitchens—removing processed foods, recommending essential meal-prep tools, and setting them up for a successful new start.

Prioritizing her own well-being, Esme embraced Pilates, relishing the subtle yet challenging small, repetitive movements. This led to deep tissue massage sessions that promoted lymphatic drainage, reduced inflammation, and boosted immune function. She established a solid routine, focusing on improving her sleep habits and tuning into her natural circadian rhythm.[11] Regular adjustments from her chiropractor addressed slight but significant spinal misalignments. She began studying the subject in depth, learning how spinal subluxations can interfere with nerve function, including the vagus nerve, affecting the autonomic and parasympathetic systems. Pressure on the vagus nerve can lead to thyroid, digestive, heart, and autoimmune issues—all symptoms she was experiencing.[12,13,14] While research continues to explore the vagus nerve's role in systemic health, some integrative practitioners suggest that chiropractic care may alleviate pressure affecting nerve function.

Meanwhile, she spearheaded a family project back in the Basque Country—converting a barn into a retreat center offering cultural experiences and fostering community wellness. Guests could enjoy local activities like hiking, cycling, boating, water-skiing, foodie tours, writing retreats, or simply unwind. They even offered a "shepherding experience," where visitors learned to shear and milk sheep, watch intelligent sheepdogs at work, and make cheese. This became a favorite among families with young children, creating lifelong memories. Moreover, the retreat attracted more visitors to the region, boosting local businesses, and as a result, Esme became a bit of a celebrity in her own right.

By centering wellness in her lifestyle and business, Esme discovered that true success comes from honoring her rhythms—not rushing through them. Her energy inspired others because it stemmed from balance, not burnout.

Case Study:

Hiroshi, Business Analyst in Tokyo, Japan - Finding Sanctuary at the Koyasan Monastery

Nestled in the serene peaks of Mount Koya in Japan, the ancient Koyasan monastery is a focal point of Zen teachings, celebrated for its commitment to harmonizing the spiritual and mundane. This sacred site, with its tranquil gardens and timeworn temples, welcomed seekers like Hiroshi, a former corporate business analyst, who had long been ensnared in the relentless demands of Tokyo's urban life.

Hiroshi arrived at Koyasan, drawn by its promise of tranquility and balance—a sanctuary from the frantic pace that characterized his career in Tokyo's high-stakes corporate environment. Here, surrounded by the silence of forested hills, he embarked on a transformative journey into the heart of Zen philosophy.

The Practice of Mindfulness and Equanimity

At Koyasan, Hiroshi immersed himself in the daily regimen of "zazen," or seated meditation, under the guidance of the monastery's wise abbot. Each meditation session was an exercise in mindfulness, teaching Hiroshi to channel his focus inward and embrace the simplicity of presence. This practice enabled him to release the frenetic thoughts that had cluttered his mind, cultivating clarity and calm that he carried beyond the meditation cushion.

Through "samu," or work as meditation, Hiroshi engaged in the monastery's daily tasks—tending to ancient gardens, preparing meals with reverence, and maintaining the sacred grounds. These activities were more than chores; they were lessons in balance, blending labor with mindfulness, each act performed with intention and care.

Integrating Balance and Clarity

The essence of Koyasan's teachings on balance was reflected in the monks' approach to integrating their spiritual lives with daily practice. Here, Hiroshi learned to set clear boundaries. A skill applied in the corporate world, he now used it to safeguard time for meditation and reflection. By balancing communal duties with solitary contemplation, he discovered the beauty of living harmoniously, where each moment became an opportunity to cultivate inner peace.

A Return to the World with New Insight

As Hiroshi practiced mindfulness and simplicity, he began to think more clearly, react more calmly, and navigate life with newfound ease. Armed with clarity and tranquility, he re-entered city life, applying Zen principles to his professional and personal interactions. He became a living embodiment of the harmony achievable through the thoughtful integration of ancient wisdom and modern existence.

Hiroshi's journey illustrates that even in high-pressure environments, stillness and structure can coexist. Let's explore how you can bring this harmony into your own life using practical, mindful tools.

Review and Implement

Creating a visual diagram to help you visualize work-life-self balance can be beneficial. Picture your responsibilities on a balance beam, with you at the center, shifting weight as needed to keep everything steady.

To put this concept into action, start by identifying your top three life priorities. Perhaps they include personal health, career advancement, or family time. Decide on a self-care action that supports each priority. If personal health is a focus, commit to a daily exercise routine. If career advancement is important, establish boundaries for your work hours. For family time, schedule weekly dinners to nurture those relationships. Set specific, actionable goals for each priority to tackle over the next week.

Recognize that this balance often shifts with the seasons of our lives and can vary for each individual and circumstance; what suits one person or phase might not work for another. As life evolves, priorities may change, requiring thoughtful choices about what aligns with your happiness and goals. Acknowledge these shifts and be open to recalibrating your approach. Achieving balance is a fluid, ongoing process of re-evaluation and adjustment that can lead to both personal and professional fulfillment.

Setting Boundaries: Sample Scripts for Saying No

To a Colleague:

"Thanks for considering me for this project. I'm currently focused on wrapping up a few commitments and won't be able to give this the attention it deserves right now. Let's explore how we might share the workload."

To a Friend:

"I appreciate the invite! I have personal commitments to attend to, so I won't be able to join this time. I'm looking forward to our next get-together."

To Family:

"I love spending time together, but I also need to protect some quiet space this week to recharge. Let's choose another day soon that works for both of us."

Clarify Your Mission - Unleash Your Potential

Quick Checklist

Exercise: Identifying Priorities and Aligning Self-Care Practices

Identify Your Top Three Priorities

Take a moment to list what truly matters to you right now. Consider areas such as career, family, health, or personal development.

Align with Self-Care Practices

For each priority, brainstorm one actionable self-care practice you can integrate into your routine.

Priority 1: [Your Priority]

Self-Care Practice: [Action]

Priority 2: [Your Priority]

Self-Care Practice: [Action]

Priority 3: [Your Priority]

Self-Care Practice: [Action]

Block out specific times in your daily or weekly calendar for self-care activities. If something feels overwhelming or unrealistic, adjust by reducing frequency, shortening the time commitment, or trying a simpler alternative.

With a new sense of balance, we're now ready to explore the time-honored traditions that nourish the mind, body, and spirit—reminders that ancient wisdom can still illuminate modern life.

CHAPTER 6

WISDOM FROM ANCIENT WELLNESS TRADITIONS

Case Study:

Emily, Digital Marketer in New York City, USA - Implementing Ayurvedic Principles

In the fast-paced world of digital marketing, where screens dictate success, Emily, a professional based in New York City, found herself battling the adverse effects of digital stress. She loved New York, a major international hub for marketing and advertising, attracting the best in the industry. However, late nights glued to her computer, constant notifications, and the blurring boundaries between work and personal time fueled her anxiety and sapped her focus. Recognizing the impact on her well-being, Emily sought a holistic remedy to restore balance and vitality to her life.

Intrigued by Ayurvedic principles, Emily began her exploration by consulting an Ayurvedic practitioner who tailored a health plan specific to her Dosha—primarily Vata, characterized by movement and change, which was exacerbating her stress levels. This personalized approach helped Emily discover a more grounded, mindful rhythm to her daily life—one that honored her body's needs rather than her inbox notifications.

Implementing Ayurvedic Habits

With guidance, Emily transitioned to an Ayurvedic lifestyle focusing on grounding practices designed to balance her Vata Dosha. Her journey emphasized routine, which was crucial for tempering Vata's irregular nature. She structured her day with consistent wake-up and sleep times, integrating gentle yoga and meditation sessions to foster stability and calm.

Nutritionally, Emily adopted a diet rich in warm, easily digestible foods, favoring seasonal vegetables and spices like cumin and turmeric to enhance digestion and clear mental fog. These dietary changes were complemented by the ritualistic use of sesame oil for Abhyanga (self-massage), which alleviated her stress and promoted physical relaxation.

Harnessing the Power of Routine

Additionally, she embraced daily Ayurvedic practices that brought mindfulness into her digital interactions. She introduced scheduled "digital detoxes," where she disconnected from her devices to reconnect with nature or enjoy a physical book. These breaks from digital noise gave her space to recharge, helping her return to work with greater clarity and calm.

Emily's newfound routines soon yielded significant improvements. Her anxiety diminished, clarity returned, and she regained control over her concentration both at work and in personal settings. The ease with which she transitioned back to a state of calm under stress underscored the integration of Ayurvedic practices as natural complements to counteracting the challenges of the digital era.

Emily's journey illustrates how creating structure—through routine, nutrition, and intentional digital breaks—can protect mental clarity in an overstimulated world. Her success inspired others to recognize that even simple habits grounded in ancient wisdom can bring lasting peace.

Case Study:

Anya, Tai Chi Master in Willowbrook, USA - A Community's Embrace of Tai Chi

In the picturesque town of Willowbrook, Illinois, nestled among rolling hills and lush greenery, a transformation began to unfold within its community. For many years, residents had been searching for ways to address rising stress levels and physical inactivity that accompanied contemporary life. The solution emerged in the gentle and rhythmic movements of Tai Chi.

This change was spearheaded by Anya Leclerc, a former Willowbrook resident and now a Tai Chi master, who decided to return to her cherished hometown. Having experienced significant benefits from Tai Chi on her health and wellness, Anya felt inspired to share these advantages with her community. To her, Tai Chi was much more than physical movement—it was a pathway to inner peace, energy, and mindful living.

Anya organized a complimentary weekend class in the town's central park, welcoming everyone—regardless of age or fitness level. Initially, only a small group of curious individuals attended, tentatively following Anya's elegant movements. Yet, word quickly spread throughout Willowbrook. As residents began to notice the calmness and energy boosts they experienced, participation swelled, attracting people from every part of town.

The Transformation Takes Hold

Soon, daily Tai Chi sessions became a town tradition, drawing people of all ages into a shared space for healing and connection.

The impact was profound. Regular Tai Chi practice significantly enhanced the physical and mental health of its practitioners. Older adults reported improved balance and flexibility, aiding in fall prevention. Office workers found relief from persistent back pain and stress-induced migraines, while children used Tai Chi as a calming method amid academic and social pressures.

Forging Stronger Community Connections

Beyond individual health improvements, Tai Chi strengthened community bonds. Each session concluded with participants sharing tea and conversation, fostering friendships that transcended generational and professional divides. Anya emerged as a beloved figure in Willowbrook, with her classes symbolizing the town's commitment to holistic health and harmonious living.

As the seasons cycled through, the residents of Willowbrook celebrated how an ancient practice could yield contemporary benefits. Tai Chi not only enhanced personal health but also fostered unity within the community. People found comfort in the practice, knowing that in the face of life's challenges, they could return to the park—breathe in sync, move collectively, and rediscover balance and peace within themselves.

Willowbrook's experience with Tai Chi reflects a common understanding among many cultures: wellness flourishes when mind, body, and spirit are honored in unison. Let's explore the enduring principles that connect these traditions.

Commonalities Among Ancient Wellness Traditions

Interconnectedness of Mind, Body, and Spirit:

Nearly all ancient health systems, from Ayurveda in India to Traditional Chinese Medicine (TCM) in China, stress the importance of harmonizing mind, body, and spirit. They advocate for a balanced approach where each element is nurtured for optimal health.

Emphasis on Balance and Harmony:

The concept of balance is pivotal, whether it's the Yin and Yang in TCM or the Tridoshas (Vata, Pitta, Kapha) in Ayurveda. These systems view health as a dynamic equilibrium that requires constant adjustment in response to lifestyle, environment, and internal changes.

Use of Natural Remedies and Elements:

These traditions recognize that nature provides the tools we need to heal and thrive—through food, plants, minerals, and the rhythms of the earth.

Preventive Approach:

Prevention takes precedence over cure, focusing on sustaining health through lifestyle practices, dietary regulation, and regular detoxification. This proactive approach aims to address ailments early by maintaining body equilibrium.

Holistic Diagnostics:

Diagnostic processes in traditions like TCM involve a comprehensive understanding of an individual's lifestyle, emotional state, and physical condition, fostering a personalized approach to healthcare. For instance, a practitioner might examine tongue color and pulse quality while inquiring about sleep patterns and stress levels to identify energy imbalances and tailor treatments accordingly.

Integration of Physical and Mental Practices:

Mind-body practices such as yoga, meditation, Tai Chi, and Qigong are integral to many ancient traditions, combining physical exercise with mental discipline to promote holistic well-being.

Community and Connection:

Traditional healing relies on community—shared rituals and collective practices forge social bonds that nurture wellness and recovery. Consider joining a healthy potluck, local meditation circle, Tai Chi class, or community garden— shared wellness experiences not only support physical health but also build meaningful connections.

These timeless insights offer a reliable compass for modern wellness, helping us find balance, clarity, and connection amid everyday chaos.

Establish Your Rituals - Cultivate Consistency

Quick Checklist

Modern Day Challenges and How They Can Be Addressed with Ancient Practices

In today's world, we face modern challenges that ancient practices address beautifully.

Digital Overwhelm: In an always-on world, constant connectivity breeds stress and fatigue. Set technology-free periods in the morning and evening to create boundaries—use this time for analog rituals like journaling or nature walks to help reset the mind.

- Ancient Solution:

  - **Mindful Practice:** Inspired by meditation practices from Buddhism, take regular digital detoxes by setting specific daily technology-free times.
  - **Rituals:** Establish morning and evening routines involving technology-free time, such as journaling or quiet reflection, drawing from ancient rituals that encourage calm and focus.

Sedentary Lifestyle: Our technology-driven habits lead to a lack of physical activity. Incorporating Yoga or Tai Chi can break this pattern by improving joint mobility, strengthening muscles, and enhancing mental focus—ideal for countering the effects of a desk-bound day.

- Ancient Solution:

  o Movement Practices: Integrate daily routines from Yoga or Tai Chi to promote physical activity and enhance energy flow.

  o **Community Engagement:** Participate in group activities or community classes reminiscent of ancient communal practices to encourage regular movement.

Lack of Connection to Nature: Urban living often disconnects individuals from nature, impacting mental health.

- Ancient Solution:

  o **Nature-based Rituals:** Set aside time for forest bathing, mindful walks, or tending to a garden or houseplants—drawing on Indigenous and agrarian traditions to ground the spirit and rejuvenate the mind.

Chronic Stress: The relentless pace of modern life and a sense of lack of control over one's destiny lead to persistent stress. Calming breathing techniques from Pranayama or Qigong can aid relaxation and stress management.

- Ancient Solution:

  o **Breathing Techniques:** Utilize deep breathing exercises from Pranayama to manage stress and enhance relaxation.

- **Holistic Health Practices:** Incorporate elements of Ayurveda and TCM, such as dietary adjustments and herbal remedies, to support stress reduction, focusing on overall balance and moderation.

As we conclude this chapter, let's carry the stillness and wisdom of these traditions forward into practical steps that can bring more peace, energy, and joy to our everyday lives.

CHAPTER 7

ACTIONABLE WELLNESS STRATEGIES

Case Study:

Laura, Software Engineer in San Francisco, USA - Transformation Through Consistency

In the heart of San Francisco, where the pace of life matches the city's vibrant energy, Laura, a dedicated software engineer, found herself at a crossroads. Juggling long hours at a tech startup with personal commitments had driven her to exhaustion. Her once-boundless enthusiasm was overshadowed by fatigue and stress, prompting her to seek a solution that would restore balance and vitality to her life.

Recognizing the need for change, Laura embraced a set of daily wellness strategies, drawing on both ancient practices and modern insights to recalibrate her life. She started with a consistent morning routine that included fifteen minutes of meditation and deep breathing exercises to center her mind and energize her day. This practice offered Laura a much-needed mental respite and set a positive tone for the daily challenges of tech life.

Implementing Small, Consistent Changes

Laura gradually integrated additional wellness strategies into her routine. She committed to a nutritious diet based on whole foods, incorporating vibrant fruits, vegetables, and lean proteins into her meals. These dietary changes significantly enhanced her energy levels and improved her concentration, enabling her to work more efficiently and creatively.

Laura made room for movement in her daily life, whether through stretch breaks at work or evening walks in Golden Gate Park. These moments of physical activity and nature immersion became essential for reducing stress and restoring calm.

Building a Supportive Community

Embracing wellness strategies wasn't something Laura did alone. She joined a local wellness group focused on mutual support and shared experiences. Through this community, she attended workshops on mindfulness, stress management, and work-life balance, cultivating friendships that reinforced her commitment to a healthier lifestyle.

As weeks turned into months, Laura noticed profound changes in her well-being. Her stress levels decreased, and her overall mood improved. She became more present and focused, both at work and in her personal life, allowing her to forge deeper connections with colleagues, friends, and family. Laura's transformation was holistic, positively impacting every facet of her life.

Inspired by her journey, Laura became a wellness advocate within her company, encouraging her coworkers to embrace similar habits. Her story spread, inspiring many to explore their paths to well-being, fostering a culture of health and balance within her workplace.

Laura's turning point came with a five-minute mindful-breathing ritual each morning. Swapping her habitual rush for intentional grounding set off a wave of healthier choices, proving that one simple, consistent habit can bring about lasting change. Her story reminds us that true wellness begins with commitment, not perfection.

Case Study:

Hoa and Linh, Parents in Los Angeles, USA - Embracing Holistic Health

Living in the heart of Los Angeles, the Tran family felt overwhelmed by the fast pace of urban life. Parents Hoa and Linh, along with their two children, found themselves caught in the hustle and bustle, with relentless work schedules, school demands, and digital distractions straining their health and family unity.

Linh, a nurse inspired by her interactions with alternative therapies, began advocating for a more holistic approach to their family's well-being. Determined to reclaim harmony amidst chaos, the Tran family decided to embrace holistic health principles, blending ancient wisdom with modern practices to rejuvenate their lifestyle.

A Family's Transformation: Beginning with Simple Steps

The transformation began with small, intentional steps. Every evening, the family gathered for dinner—a sacred ritual that became a time to connect, prepare wholesome foods together, and practice gratitude. These dinners turned into educational moments where Linh introduced the family to the benefits of integrating more plant-based and whole foods into their diet, drawing on both traditional Vietnamese dishes and modern nutritional insights.

Recognizing the importance of physical and emotional balance, they adopted Tai Chi as a family practice. Guided by a local instructor in a community class, this ancient martial art offered them a gentle yet powerful tool to cultivate both physical strength and emotional peace. Practicing Tai Chi together provided the Tran family not only physical benefits but also a source of shared calm, emotional bonding, and joyful connection.

Cultivating Mindfulness and Connection

In their quest for balance, the Trans integrated mindfulness practices into their daily routine. Mornings began with simple meditation exercises designed to foster awareness and calm, setting a positive tone for the day ahead. These practices taught the children, Liam and Mai, the value of presence and focus, skills that translated into improved concentration and academic performance.

The family's holistic approach extended beyond internal practices. They actively sought to reduce their environmental footprint by implementing sustainable habits at home—composting, minimizing waste, and using eco-friendly products.[1] Together they nurtured a small home garden, turning weekend mornings into hands-on learning sessions where they grew and harvested their own vegetables.

Unity Through Holistic Practices

As the months passed, the Tran family noticed a remarkable transformation. Their health improved, stress diminished, and their sense of togetherness strengthened. Linh and Hoa found their marriage growing more connected through shared goals and values, while Liam and Mai thrived, supported by the foundation of wellness and open communication at home.

Inspired by their success, Linh began sharing their journey with friends and neighbors, hosting small gatherings to raise awareness about the benefits of holistic health. This initiative sparked a growing community movement within their neighborhood, emphasizing the power of holistic health to foster wellness, sustainability, and community connections.

The Tran family's story highlights the impact of adopting holistic health principles, illustrating how these practices can transform individual health, family dynamics, and community well-being. Through intentional and communal approaches to living, they remind us all of the holistic journey's ability to nurture balanced, fulfilled lives amidst life's challenges.

Just as the Tran family embraced everyday wellness, leaders around the world are dedicating their lives to helping others access similar tools. Let's meet two visionaries who are advancing this movement at the highest levels.

Visionary: Lara Adler - Environmental Toxin Education

Lara Adler is a prominent figure in environmental health, renowned for her expertise in educating both professionals and the public about the impact of toxins on health.[2] Focusing on empowering individuals to make informed decisions, Lara combines scientific insights with practical advice, making complex environmental health topics accessible and actionable.

Specialized Knowledge in Environmental Health

- **Toxins and Public Health:** Lara educates on how everyday exposure to environmental toxins—such as chemicals in consumer products, pesticides, and industrial pollutants—can affect human health. Her work is instrumental in raising awareness about the subtle yet profound impacts these substances have on both acute and chronic health issues.

- **Educational Outreach:** Through courses, workshops, and speaking engagements, Lara disseminates knowledge on reducing toxic exposure and advocating for healthier choices. Her efforts aim to bridge the gap between scientific research and public understanding, fostering a culture of wellness enhanced by environmental awareness.

Approach and Methodology

- **Holistic Perspective:** Lara emphasizes a holistic approach to healthcare, advocating for lifestyle changes and environmental modifications that can effectively mitigate health risks. She encourages proactive health management by identifying and eliminating potential sources of toxins within homes and workplaces.

- **Expert Collaboration:** By collaborating with experts across various fields, including nutrition, medicine, and environmental science, Lara ensures her teachings are grounded in comprehensive, evidence-based research. This collaboration enhances the credibility and applicability of her educational content.

Impact and Advocacy

- **Raising Awareness:** Lara's initiatives have significantly impacted public discourse on environmental health, prompting individuals and communities to reconsider their daily habits and push for regulatory changes. Her work inspires a movement towards greater transparency in product ingredient labeling and safer environmental practices.

Lara empowers individuals to adopt toxin-free lifestyles through educational programs and community outreach. Simultaneously, she collaborates with legislators and regulatory bodies to strengthen environmental health standards, advocating for greater transparency in consumer safety and ingredient labeling. By bridging personal behavior change with policy reform, she drives lasting improvements in both daily practices and systemic protections for a healthier world.

Visionary: Dr. Ritamarie Loscalzo - Institute of Nutritional Endocrinology

Dr. Ritamarie Loscalzo is a leading expert in functional medicine, known for her commitment to holistic health education and innovative wellness solutions.[3] With over three decades of clinical experience, she specializes in natural methods for addressing hormonal imbalances, digestive issues, and enhancing energy levels. Dr. Ritamarie is a licensed Doctor of Chiropractic, complemented by certifications in acupuncture, clinical nutrition, herbal medicine, and HeartMath®, which she applies in creating personalized strategies that tackle health issues at their root cause.[4]

As the founder of the Institute of Nutritional Endocrinology, Dr. Ritamarie dedicates herself to educating healthcare professionals, including doctors, nurses, nutrition coaches, and holistic practitioners. Her Institute equips practitioners with advanced tools to support patients dealing with complex conditions often underserved by conventional care.

Dr. Ritamarie actively shares her insights through workshops, seminars, and online courses, guiding others in the integration of natural therapies with clinical practices. Her prolific work as an author and speaker helps demystify complex health topics, making them accessible to a wider audience.

Her holistic approach emphasizes prevention, nutrition, and lifestyle modifications to foster sustainable health and wellness. Through her pioneering efforts, Dr. Ritamarie inspires both the healthcare community and individuals seeking natural health optimization, underscoring the impact of informed, holistic care.

Review and Implement

Commit to Action - Sustain Your Momentum

Quick Checklist

Dietary Adjustments

Consider opting for a diet rich in whole, fresh organic foods while consciously avoiding packaged, canned, and frozen products, as well as GMO-based and processed items. Eliminate dairy, gluten, corn, sugar, soy, coffee, soda, and alcohol for a period to help your body reset to its natural, balanced state. Gradually, you'll begin craving more wholesome foods, and the desire for junk food will wane. Combining this dietary shift with adequate sleep, regular exercise, plenty of water, and relaxation can significantly boost your health.

A couple of sample meals are provided below, suitable for a generally healthy individual. For those with chronic health issues requiring additional deep-dive support, these samples may require fine-tuning.

1. Sample Meal Plan - Introductory

- **Breakfast:** Overnight oats with chia seeds, almond milk, berries, and a drizzle of honey.
- **Lunch:** Grilled chicken salad with mixed greens, cherry tomatoes, cucumber, avocado, and vinaigrette.

- **Dinner:** Baked salmon with lemon and herbs, served with quinoa and steamed broccoli.
- **Snacks:** A handful of nuts or a piece of fruit.

2. Sample Meal Plan – with Protein Options and Ginger Sauce Recipe

- **Breakfast:** Avocado toast on sourdough bread, topped with sliced tomatoes, a pinch of sea salt, and lemon juice, accompanied by a smoothie made with spinach, banana, and almond milk.
- **Lunch:** Quinoa and black bean salad with fresh cilantro, cherry tomatoes, and lime vinaigrette. Pair with a protein option (grilled chicken, lentils, or chickpeas) based on dietary preferences.

Legumes: lentils, chickpeas, black beans, kidney beans

- **Dinner:** Stir-fried vegetables such as bell peppers, broccoli, and snow peas, tossed in a black bean and ginger sauce *(recipe below)*. Pair with grilled salmon or a plant-based protein option like quinoa, chia seeds, or walnuts.
- **Snacks:** Sliced cucumbers with hummus or a small bowl of mixed berries. Enjoy a handful of almonds or walnuts for an afternoon energy boost.

Sample Black Bean and Ginger Sauce

This versatile sauce combines the umami of fermented black beans with the warmth of ginger, the depth of garlic, and the brightness of rice vinegar—perfect for enhancing any vegetable or protein dish. It's a delicious alternative to sesame and ginger sauce for those allergic to sesame and/or nuts.

- **Fermented Black Beans:** The heart of the sauce, these beans provide an umami-rich flavor that forms the foundation.
- **Ginger:** Adds a spicy bite and invigorating aroma, contributing warmth to the overall profile.
- **Green Onions:** Provide a mild onion flavor, balancing the sauce with their fresh taste.
- **Rice Vinegar:** Offers a delicate, sweet tang that harmonizes the sauce.
- **Chinese Rice Wine:** Known for its aromatic quality and slightly sweet, briny flavor, adding complexity.
- **Garlic:** Delivers a potent combination of pungency and umami, along with subtle sweetness, enhancing the sauce's depth.
- **Sea Salt:** A pinch enhances the overall flavors without overpowering them.
- **Hot Pepper Sauce:** Introduces a contrasting kick, tying everything together with a touch of heat.

Detoxification and Cleansing Programs

Detoxification and fasting are rooted in various traditions and religions worldwide, reflecting a blend of spiritual and health purposes.[5] In ancient Egypt, detox was intertwined with spiritual rituals, utilizing cleansing herbs to rejuvenate the body. Ayurveda in India advocates fasting to balance bodily energies and promote spiritual clarity. Ancient Greeks, including Hippocrates, recognized the body's self-healing capabilities, recommending fasting for health restoration.

Different religions highlight fasting and detox as pathways to spiritual growth and purification. Judaism observes fasting during Yom Kippur and other significant events, symbolizing atonement and spiritual renewal. Christianity promotes fasting as a method of penance and spiritual focus, particularly during Lent. In Islam, fasting during Ramadan represents purification, self-discipline, and empathy for the less fortunate.

Buddhism incorporates fasting to cultivate mindfulness and inner peace, while Hinduism regards it as a means to attain spiritual discipline. Shintoism views purification rituals, including fasting, as vital for spiritual cleanliness. Native American cultures use sweat lodges for physical and spiritual cleansing. Natural Hygiene practices emphasize the body's innate ability to heal through fasting and detox.

In Traditional Chinese Medicine (TCM), detoxification maintains the flow of Qi, essential for health and vitality. Herbal medicine often accompanies detoxes to cleanse the body, emphasizing holistic healing. Historical detox practices collectively underscore the importance of maintaining health and balance, forming a diverse, enduring framework for modern wellness strategies.

Detoxing for Generally Healthy Individuals

Autophagy, an essential biological process, involves the body's cellular system breaking down and recycling damaged cells. For generally healthy individuals, this state offers various benefits, playing a critical role in cellular maintenance, longevity, and disease prevention.

Benefits of Autophagy for Healthy Individuals

1. **Cellular Renewal:** Autophagy helps remove damaged or dysfunctional cellular components, promoting healthy cell regeneration and improving overall function. This process supports tissue health and longevity, essential for maintaining youthful vigor.

2. **Metabolic Health:** Autophagy cleans out and recycles damaged cells, enabling the body to use energy more efficiently. This boost to metabolism can support healthy weight management and lower the risk of conditions like diabetes and obesity.

3. **Inflammation Reduction:** Autophagy mitigates inflammation by clearing out damaged cells that

contribute to inflammatory processes. This effect supports overall immune function and may help protect against chronic diseases associated with inflammation, such as arthritis.

4. **Neuroprotection:** In the brain, autophagy is instrumental in clearing damaged proteins and mitochondria, reducing the risks of neurodegenerative diseases like Alzheimer's and Parkinson's. By preserving neural health, it supports cognitive function and mental acuity.

5. **Longevity and Anti-Aging:** Regular autophagy contributes to longer lifespans and delays the onset of age-related declines by maintaining cellular integrity. It helps the body cope with stress and environmental factors, potentially enhancing quality of life as one ages.

Incorporating habits that support autophagy—such as movement and mindful eating—can help keep your body running smoothly and feeling its best over time. Maintaining a balanced lifestyle that encourages autophagy can significantly contribute to overall well-being.

Simple practices like intermittent fasting and regular movement promote cellular renewal and may support healthier aging.

The Research

There is ongoing debate among scientists regarding the benefits and risks of detoxing and fasting, with valid points raised on both sides.[6] Supporters argue that these practices help the body eliminate toxins, promote digestive health, clear out accumulated waste, and improve energy levels. Skeptics caution against potential risks, noting that some detox regimens can disrupt nutrient balance or lead to dehydration and health issues if not conducted properly.

It is important to consult reputable sources and healthcare professionals when considering such programs. An informed approach, grounded in reliable advice, ensures that detox efforts align with personal health needs and safeguard well-being.

An ongoing study at the Massachusetts Institute of Technology (MIT) recently revealed findings indicating that short-term caloric restriction and fasting can aid intestinal stem cell regeneration and healing, while long-term fasting may be less beneficial. Returning to a regular eating regimen after a prolonged fasting period must be done slowly and cautiously to avoid over-regeneration of stem cells during this crucial time.

While fasting can offer short-term benefits for many, it may not be ideal for everyone. An alternative or complementary approach involves adopting healthy lifestyle habits and a clean, organic diet to support the body's natural regeneration cycles. Incorporating stem cell-friendly foods can significantly enhance natural cell growth. Cruciferous vegetables like cauliflower, watercress, kale, cabbage, broccoli, Brussels sprouts, and bok choy are particularly effective in promoting stem cell growth.[7]

Mushrooms such as shiitake and maitake are rich in polyphenols, essential micronutrients for cellular health. Similarly, olive oil high in polyphenols—especially from arid regions like Morocco—is prized for its antioxidant properties.

Berries—including blueberries, raspberries, goji berries, and pomegranate—enhance superoxide dismutase (SOD), a powerful antioxidant. Seeds and nuts serve as convenient, protein-rich snacks, while seafood and fatty fish deliver omega-3 fatty acids, natural activators of adult stem cells.

If you're unsure where to begin, here are a few small but impactful practices to kickstart your wellness journey.

Choose Wellness Practices

- **Mindfulness:** Practice deep breathing for 2 minutes.
- **Hydration:** Drink a glass of water after waking up.
- **Movement:** Do a 5-minute stretch routine.

To make new habits stick, try pairing them with routines you already practice. This technique, known as habit-stacking, helps make change feel more natural.

Habit-Stacking

Habit-stacking is a strategy that links a new wellness habit to an established daily routine, making it easier to incorporate and maintain.[9]

Habit-Stacking Strategy

- Morning Routine:

  - After brushing your teeth, practice deep breathing.
  - After making coffee, drink a glass of water.

- Lunchtime:

  - Follow lunch with a 10-minute walk or stretching routine before returning to work.

- Evening Wind-Down:

  - After dinner, engage in a calming activity like reading or journaling to signal your body to relax before bedtime.
  - Before watching TV, perform a 5-minute stretch.

Commit and Reward

- Set reminders to keep new habits on track.

- Reward yourself with something enjoyable—like extra leisure time, a relaxing bath, or a special outing—after maintaining your new habit for a week.

The upcoming chapter unveils effective strategies for weaving mindfulness into your everyday life, enhancing mental clarity and emotional balance. Discover how mindfulness serves as both a foundational and transformative force, enriching your holistic health journey with nuanced awareness and intentional living. Are you ready to embark on a path toward greater vitality and equilibrium?

CHAPTER 8

INTEGRATING MINDFULNESS INTO HOLISTIC HEALTH

Case Study:

Ram and Anjali, Parents in Mumbai, India - Integrating Ayurveda and Meditation

In the bustling city of Mumbai, the Reddy family faced the fast-paced demands of urban living and decided to embark on a transformative journey toward holistic health. Ram, a software engineer, and his wife Anjali, a schoolteacher, recognized the rising stress and fatigue their demanding schedules imposed—not only on themselves but also on their children, Ravi and Sita.

Determined to forge a healthier path, they embraced Ayurveda and meditation, integrating these ancient practices into their daily lives to foster physical wellness and a harmonious home environment.

Embracing an Ayurvedic Lifestyle

The family's journey began with a consultation from an Ayurvedic practitioner, who created personalized wellness plans tailored to their individual constitutions, known as Doshas. Ram's Vata imbalance and Anjali's tendency towards Pitta required specific dietary adjustments and lifestyle changes.

They incorporated Ayurvedic principles into their diets, focusing on fresh, seasonal produce and traditional Indian dishes rich in spices like turmeric and ginger, known for their anti-inflammatory properties. Morning routines included oil pulling and sipping warm herbal teas to improve oral health, support digestion, and provide a calm, grounded start to the day.

Integrating Meditation and Mindfulness

Alongside these dietary changes, the Reddy family adopted daily meditation practices. Each morning began with a group meditation session, where gentle guidance through breathing exercises and focused relaxation set a calm and centered tone for the day. This shared morning ritual deepened their emotional connection, making the household feel more harmonious throughout the day.

To further solidify these gains, weekly family yoga sessions became a cherished tradition, blending physical activity with mindfulness, enhancing flexibility, strength, and unity.

A Harmonious and Supportive Environment

The gradual adoption of these holistic practices led to remarkable improvements in the Reddys' lives. Ram experienced reduced work-related stress and greater mental clarity, while Anjali found renewed energy and equilibrium in her dual roles at home and school. The children's academic performance and interpersonal relationships thrived within this supportive environment.

The Reddy family's daily mindfulness and Ayurvedic practices revitalized their lives with deeper calm, focus, and connection, inspiring friends and neighbors to pursue well-being in their own homes. They began hosting workshops, sharing practical insights and personal experiences, becoming trusted guides in their community and sparking individual growth and a collective embrace of mindful, health-centered living.

Case Study:

Dana Thompson, Educator in Seattle, USA - Introducing Mindfulness to Support Students

In a bustling school in Seattle, Dana Thompson, a passionate educator committed to nurturing her students' well-being, embarked on a unique personal journey. Recognizing the mounting stress, distractions, and emotional challenges her students faced, Dana sought innovative ways to create a more harmonious classroom environment. Inspired by traditional Buddhist practices and contemporary psychological research, she decided to integrate mindfulness techniques into her teaching.

Introducing Mindfulness in Education

At the start of a new academic year, Dana introduced her students to simple mindfulness exercises. Each morning began with a few minutes of silent reflection, guided breathing exercises, and activities designed to focus attention and cultivate calmness. Dana made it fun and age-appropriate by having students imagine their breaths as rising balloons or feeling rooted like trees, engaging their imaginations and making mindfulness accessible.

These sessions encouraged students to tune into the present moment, setting a focused and peaceful tone for the rest of the day. Students practiced taking turns speaking while others listened attentively—an exercise that built mutual respect and sharpened their focus.

By integrating these techniques, Dana created a classroom culture grounded in respect and attentiveness, fostering an atmosphere of mutual understanding and cooperation.

Significant Improvements in Students

Within weeks, Dana's mindfulness lessons translated into sharper focus, calmer classrooms, and stronger self-regulation—shy students spoke up with confidence, and energetic ones channeled their vitality productively.

Academically, students became more engaged in learning, with better focus and improved task completion—benefits that extended beyond the mindfulness sessions. Inspired by these results, Dana collaborated with colleagues to expand mindfulness school-wide, engaging parents who reported calmer, more reflective behavior at home.

Embracing a Culture of Mindfulness

Dana's mindfulness program became a model for schools across the district, weaving time-honored practices with modern psychology to foster both academic excellence and emotional growth. Her work demonstrates how integrating mindfulness builds resilience and emotional intelligence, equipping students with lifelong tools for success and well-being.

Dana's classroom story illustrates mindfulness in action—but what's happening in the brain when we practice? Let's explore the science behind these transformative effects.

Review and Implement

Mindfulness and meditation produce significant neurobiological changes that enhance emotional regulation and mental clarity. A prime example is the impact on the amygdala, a brain region essential for processing emotions such as fear and stress.[1] Studies indicate that regular meditation can reduce the size and activity level of the amygdala, leading to increased emotional resilience and a calmer mindset. This demonstrates how consistent mindfulness can reshape parts of the brain, fostering greater calm and emotional balance.

The potential benefits are particularly notable for individuals struggling with subtle yet impactful brain damage, possibly due to a physical blow, affecting the amygdala.[2] Such practices hold promise for those navigating complex emotional or cognitive challenges, including individuals in institutional care settings.[3]

Optimize Your Efforts - Elevate Your Impact

Quick Checklist

Monthly Mindfulness Reflection

Mindfulness extends beyond our inner world—it influences how we speak, listen, and relate to others. This section encourages you to reflect on how awareness shapes communication.

Use this gentle self-check to assess how mindfulness is manifesting in your life. There's no 'perfect score'—just insight into your growth and areas that merit more attention.

Mindfulness Integration Self-Assessment	Score 1-5	Notes
Daily Presence		
I can stay focused on the present moment without distraction.		
I regularly pause to take deep breaths during my day.		
I mindfully engage in my routines (e.g., eating, walking).		
Emotional Awareness		
I am aware of my emotional responses in different situations.		
I can identify and name my emotions as they arise.		
I use mindfulness practices to manage stress and emotion.		
Reaction to Stress		
I notice early signs of stress and respond with mindfulness techniques.		

Mindfulness Integration Self-Assessment	Score 1-5	Notes
I utilize meditation or breathing exercises when faced with stress.		
I maintain calm and center myself in high-pressure situations.		
Mindful Communication		
I listen actively and attentively in conversations, without interrupting.		
I express myself thoughtfully and with awareness of my words' impact.		
I actively listen to others' perspectives with openness and empathy.		
Overall Mindfulness Practices		
I dedicate time daily to formal mindfulness practices like meditation.		
I recognize improvements in my well-being due to mindfulness.		
I actively seek to learn and improve my mindfulness skills.		

In the next chapter, we'll explore how simple rituals—morning routines, reflective pauses, and evening wind-downs—can anchor you in meaning, presence, and self-awareness.

CHAPTER 9

CREATING PERSONAL WELL-BEING RITUALS

Case Study:

Lily, Artist in Miami, USA - Dwindling Creativity Due to Constant Deadlines

In the vibrant cultural landscape of Miami, Lily, a renowned artist known for her canvases filled with vivid imagery and bold hues, faced an unexpected challenge: a creative block. Living amidst the architectural beauty of Miami's Art Deco district, her art celebrated the eclectic spirit of the city. However, as constant deadlines loomed, her creative spark began to fade, prompting Lily to reassess her routine and seek rejuvenation.

Designing Her Well-Being Rituals

To reignite her creativity, Lily crafted personalized well-being rituals that aligned her artistic pursuits with self-discovery. Each morning, she awoke to the gentle rustle of palm trees, engaging in meditation and gratitude journaling. These moments, bathed in the warm Miami sunrise, became her sanctuary, nurturing her mind and setting a positive tone for her creative day.

Lily found joy in preparing healthy lunches in her brightly lit kitchen, where blending vibrant tones and textures became a therapeutic ritual that refreshed her mind and lifted her spirit. As she cooked, a playlist of Latin rhythms and jazz melodies energized her creativity and grounded her emotions.

Afternoon Adventures and Creative Inspiration

In the afternoons, Lily often strolled along the Venetian Causeway, where the rhythmic sounds of ocean waves and lively local chatter sparked fresh inspiration. Her walks led her past hand-painted murals and bustling open-air markets, deepening her appreciation for Miami's everyday beauty.

A favorite stop on her journey was Café Cubano, a quaint café tucked away off Ocean Drive, where she regularly met friends for Cuban espresso and spirited conversations. Moments like these enriched her sense of community, fostering connections amidst the vibrant city buzz.

On her return home, Lily often visited 'Books & Books,' an independent bookstore just a short walk from her home. Browsing the aisles for a new novel, she found comfort in diving into worlds of fiction. The bookstore wasn't just a literary haven; it was also a neighborhood hub where Lily met kindred spirits, swapping stories that often found their way into her art.

Embracing Miami's Cultural Tapestry

In the evenings, Lily unwound with her latest novel, allowing narratives to whisk her away to distant worlds. Each page opened new realms of relaxation and sparked imaginative ideas for her art, enriching her creative flow.

On weekends, Lily laced up her boots for hiking the winding boardwalks of Everglades National Park or mounted her bike for the shaded trails of Oleta River State Park. Among towering mangroves, brilliant orchids, and the chatter of wading birds, she found a peaceful refuge. The rush of fresh air and kaleidoscope of wildlife reignited her creative spark, enabling her to return to her studio with a clear mind and a canvas full of new ideas.

Miami's cultural depth offered endless opportunities for local and international talent, and Lily made it a point to attend a concert or event at least once a month. The Miami City Ballet often provided free impromptu pop-up performances for the local community, always a delight, and Lily would be there in the crowd whenever she could. The pulsating energy of live music performances and art exhibitions reinvigorated her spirit, re-aligning her with the heartbeat of the city she adored.

A Journey Towards Fulfillment

These intentional rituals reshaped Lily's creative process and enriched her life. With each passing day, her stress dissipated while her artwork flourished, embodying a renewed vitality that resonated on every canvas. Her rituals didn't just reduce stress; they reignited her creativity, infusing her artwork with new life, color, and emotional depth.

Case Study:

Hannah, Political Reporter in Washington, D.C., USA - From Tight Deadlines to Serenity

In the bustling epicenter of Washington, D.C., Hannah, a tenacious political reporter, found herself engulfed by the relentless news cycle. Her days were defined by tight deadlines, ceaseless updates, and constant pressure to deliver the next big scoop. This high-stakes environment, while thrilling, took a toll on her health and happiness, resulting in chronic stress and mounting fatigue.

Recognizing the need for change, Hannah embarked on a journey to create personal well-being rituals that could restore balance and serenity to her demanding life. Inspired by the wellness trends and mental health stories she covered, she decided to implement these insights into her daily routine.

Mapping Out New Rituals

Hannah began her transformation by carving out quiet moments in her schedule for personal rejuvenation. Early mornings, once consumed by hurried coffee and news briefings, became times for reflection. She adopted a ten-minute mindfulness practice, focusing on her breath and body awareness, cultivating calm before diving into the day's challenges.

Just as mindfulness helped her greet the day with intention, Hannah rethought how she fueled her body. Food, which had once been a hurried afterthought, became a ritual of conscious nourishment. She embraced meal prep on Sunday afternoons, cooking dishes for the hectic week ahead. These culinary sessions turned into a relaxing exercise of creativity, offering a refreshing contrast to her intellectually demanding, often overthinking professional life.

To balance her professional obligations with personal time, Hannah established digital detox evenings. She set aside her phone and laptop, opting instead for a walk in a nearby park or an hour of light reading, allowing her mind to wander and unwind naturally.

Building a Network of Support

Key to Hannah's journey was surrounding herself with a supportive network. She joined a local wellness group that met weekly to share experiences and support each other's health goals. These gatherings not only offered fresh perspectives on managing stress; they reminded Hannah she wasn't alone. In this circle of encouragement, she felt heard, supported, and reenergized.

As Hannah integrated these rituals, she experienced a significant shift in her well-being. She navigated her days with newfound clarity and peace, resulting in improved focus, better health, and a more balanced emotional state. Her ability to manage the high-pressure demands of her job with grace and patience increased markedly, earning her both personal satisfaction and professional recognition. Hannah's story illustrates how even the most driven professionals can find harmony by intentionally redesigning their routines to foster a healthier lifestyle.

Hannah's experience is part of a much larger human narrative—one in which rituals have always helped people navigate life's demands with intention and meaning.

Review and Implement

The Enduring Role of Rituals: A Multidisciplinary Perspective

Rituals Across Time and Cultures

From ancient times to the present, rituals have been integral to the human experience. They provide meaning, define cultural identities, and enhance personal growth. Rituals possess enduring power by uniting the physical and spiritual—like lighting a candle during prayer or stretching before meditation—acts that ground us while elevating our awareness. This framework reinforces community bonds and the continuity of tradition. As a core human trait, rituals are so pervasive that exploring them necessitates a multidisciplinary approach, including anthropology, archaeology, biology, primatology, cognitive science, psychology, religious studies, and demography.[2]

Historical Significance and Cultural Identity

Originating from the Latin "ritualis," meaning "relating to rites," rituals initially marked religious and cultural activities that expressed faith, connection, and shared communal values. Ancient civilizations such as the Egyptians, Mesopotamians, and Mayans developed intricate rituals to honor their gods and guide societal norms, often linked to celestial events and agricultural cycles. For example, Mayan priests gathered at sunrise on the spring equinox at Chichén Itzá, where the serpent-shaped shadow descending the Kukulkan Pyramid marked the start of the planting season and invoked divine blessings for the harvest. The ancient Egyptians held elaborate ceremonies aligned with the flooding of the Nile and the rising of Sirius, which they regarded as divine signs of renewal and abundance.

Religious Contexts

In religious contexts, rituals provide the framework for worship, ensuring communities adhere to spiritual tenets and pass down traditions across generations. For instance, in Christianity, sacraments and liturgical practices unite believers in a shared spiritual narrative. Similarly, Hindu rituals such as Puja and Buddhist meditative rites emphasize reverence and connection to the divine.

Social and Personal Significance

Socially, rituals underscore cultural identity and cohesion. Practices like marriage ceremonies and rites of passage serve as communal affirmations of societal values and milestones. These rituals carry psychological importance, offering individuals a sense of stability, continuity, and belonging within their community. On a personal level, rituals provide structured means of expressing emotions, processing transitions, and coping with life's uncertainties. Personal rituals, such as mindfulness practices or morning routines, create a rhythm that promotes mental well-being.

The Absence of Rituals: Impacts on Individuals and Communities

The absence of rituals can leave life feeling unmoored, stripping away the structure and sense of purpose that routines provide. Without these practices to anchor our days, individuals often face disconnection, aimlessness, and heightened stress as they struggle to find predictability and meaning. Rituals facilitate the processing of life stages and transitional experiences, such as bereavement or personal growth, potentially leading to an emotional and psychological void. Communities also suffer when shared rituals disappear—cultural identity weakens, social bonds fray, and the collective support needed to navigate life's transitions vanishes, leaving both individuals and groups vulnerable to emotional and psychological imbalance.

Creating Personal Well-Being Rituals

The essence of creating personal well-being rituals lies in identifying what resonates with you. Begin by reflecting deeply on your values, which guide your life decisions, helping to carve a path toward fulfillment. Consider activities that bring you joy and help you feel grounded, whether painting, cooking, or writing. Evaluate your current lifestyle and pinpoint routines that already support your well-being—like a morning tea or evening walk. Set clear intentions for your rituals and define your goals, whether it's relaxation, creativity, or mindfulness in daily life.

Implementing these insights involves several thoughtful steps. Start by defining your top values, then identify activities that express and support those values. When your rituals reflect what matters most, they become sources of meaning—not just routine.

Track Your Milestones - Perfect Your Path

Quick Checklist

Ritual-Building Worksheet

Prompts for Identifying Meaningful Activities:

Step 1: Reflect on Your Values

- **Identify Core Values**: List your top three values (e.g., health, family, creativity, growth).
- **Evaluate Alignment:** Consider how your current habits align with these values.

Step 2: Identify Activities:

- List activities that bring you joy and fulfillment. Identify at least five.
  Example: Painting, running, cooking, meditation, writing.
- Consider activities you've enjoyed since childhood—these often reflect deep-rooted joys that still nourish us as adults.

Step 3: Align Activities with Values

- Choose activities that reflect and support your key values.
  Example: Meditation aligns with self-awareness.

Step 4: Assess Lifestyle and Needs

- **Daily Routine:** Outline a typical day, highlighting areas that need change.
- **Key Needs**: Identify your primary physical, mental, and emotional needs.

Step 5: Set Intentions:

- What do you hope to achieve with your ritual?
- How can this ritual enhance your personal well-being?

Step 6: Define Your Well-Being Rituals

Think of your day in phases—morning, midday, and evening—and create simple rituals for each that match your energy and needs.

Daily Practice

- **Morning Rituals:** List activities that energize and motivate you for the day ahead.

Examples:

- Begin with a 5-minute meditation and gratitude journaling.
- Stretch or practice yoga for 10 minutes to invigorate your body.
- **Midday Rituals:** List activities that reduce stress, encourage physical activity, and prepare you for the afternoon.

Examples:

- Take a mindful walk during lunch to reconnect with nature.
- Practice deep-breathing exercises to refresh focus and calm.
- **Evening Rituals:** List activities that help you unwind and relax.

Examples:

- Dedicate time to reading or reflection.
- Engage in a relaxation routine like a warm bath or calming music.

Step 7: Weekly Practice:

- Select an activity to engage in at least once a week.

Step 8: Determine Timing

- Allocate specific times for each activity but remain flexible. Life shifts—what matters is keeping your rituals present, not perfect.

  Example: Painting on Saturday mornings or another preferred time during the week.

Step 9: Set Goals

- **Short-Term Goals**: Set two achievable goals for the next month related to your rituals.
- **Long-Term Vision**: Envision how these rituals can support your long-term well-being.

Step 10: Monitor and Adjust Regularly

- **Track Progress:** Keep a daily or weekly log of your rituals and their effects on your well-being.
- **Reflect and Adjust:** Revisit your rituals monthly to ensure they continue to serve you effectively and make necessary adjustments.

As we delve into the practical benefits of wellness strategies, we will now explore the role that community can play in our journey toward holistic well-being. In the next chapter, you'll meet individuals who found renewed purpose and support through community—reminding us that wellness isn't a solo journey but a shared path full of connection, strength, and joy.

CHAPTER 10

HARNESSING THE POWER OF COMMUNITY

Case Study:

Ethan, Principal Software Engineer in Sydney, Australia - Seeking Supportive Community

In Sydney's bustling metropolis, amidst its iconic skyline and vibrant tech scene, Ethan, a principal software engineer, navigated life like a solitary wanderer. Despite his commitment to wellness and the integration of IT in that space, his isolated approach became increasingly burdensome, compounded by relentless backlash from global players. Other agendas were at play—ones that prioritized profit over individual efficacy. Tired of this business model, he sought authenticity, hoping his efforts would genuinely help others and allow him to give back. Each day felt like an endurance trial, marked by fleeting moments of uncertainty and the pervasive quiet of solitude.

Driven by a desire to change his path, Ethan sought the camaraderie he realized he was missing. His journey led him to a local yoga studio nestled in Sydney's eclectic streets, a serendipitous discovery that became the catalyst for his transformation.

From Isolation to Community Connection

As Ethan stepped into the yoga studio, he was greeted with genuine warmth by the instructor and participants. The class fostered an ethos of inclusivity and collective support, making everyone feel valued and encouraged to share their experiences. For Ethan, this newfound community was both unfamiliar and comforting.

Over time, Ethan's journey took a significant turn. Each yoga session, blending mindfulness with physical exertion, enhanced his health and cultivated a rich tapestry of friendships. Through shared narratives, he discovered that his struggles were more common than he had realized and far less daunting when faced together.

Personal Growth Through Shared Experiences

In the months that followed, the nurturing yoga community became a cornerstone of Ethan's personal evolution. The relationships he formed encouraged him to explore new avenues of self-care, such as group meditation sessions and weekend retreats in Bali. These experiences expanded his understanding of wellness, enriching it with mental and emotional balance.

Every interaction within this community provided Ethan with profound insights into his life's trajectory. He learned not only from his reflections but also from the perseverance and optimism of those around him. This collective wisdom offered a strong framework of support, helping him navigate personal and professional challenges.

The Ripple Effect: Inspiring Community Growth

Revitalized and inspired, Ethan aimed to give back to the community that had enriched his life. He launched a series of wellness workshops at the studio, inviting experts to discuss various aspects of holistic health. This initiative rekindled the community's dedication to wellness, attracting a diverse array of members and spreading a message of collective prosperity.

Ethan's story reminds us that healing doesn't need to happen in isolation. When we open ourselves to connection, we find that support, inspiration, and renewal often begin in shared spaces.

Case Study:

Alex, Financial CEO in Chicago, USA - Path to Community and Wellness

In the relentless world of high finance, Alex felt suffocated by endless spreadsheets and towering deadlines. His life, once filled with the promise of success, had devolved into a monotonous cycle—a mirage of fulfillment slipping further away each day. As stress mounted and satisfaction dwindled, Alex's mind teetered toward burnout, propelling him into the depths of corporate fatigue.

During a pivotal moment of introspection amidst the chaos, Alex realized he needed to reset his trajectory. Leaving behind a promising career, he embarked on a journey to an ashram in the foothills of the Himalayas—a quest for self-discovery fueled by the hope of finding true balance.

Awakening Through Mindfulness

At the ashram, Alex's introduction to mindfulness practices like yoga and meditation was transformative. The simplicity of these routines opened a portal to inner peace he had long forgotten. Each morning began with the call of a bell, a gentle reminder of nature's cycles, drawing him into deep breathing and reflective meditation. These moments of stillness allowed Alex to peel back layers of stress and anxiety, replacing them with serenity and clarity.

As Alex engaged in mindful self-study and introspection, he experienced an internal shift. The weight of past expectations melted away, making room for acceptance and contentment. Unburdened by the demands of his former life, he developed a balanced perspective, achieving harmony between his personal and professional roles.

The Power of Community

Living among others at the ashram, each on their unique journeys, Alex discovered the strength of community. Shared stories around evening fires and collaborative daily chores fostered a sense of belonging—a stark contrast to his previous isolation. These connections nourished his soul and supported his transformation, instilling hope for a holistic lifestyle beyond the ashram's tranquil confines.

Returning with Renewed Perspective

This experience extended into an extended stay in the Himalayas, hiking and visiting villages, followed by additional time in other ashrams. Alex emerged from this inward adventure with a new perspective, ready to reintegrate into his former world. Equipped with the mindfulness and wellness practices he had internalized, he returned to his career with resilience, choosing to consult on sustainable investment projects.

This shift in focus allowed him to merge professional responsibilities with his personal ethos—balancing ambition with purpose.

Alex's ongoing commitment to his practice extends beyond personal growth; he mentors others at his firm, fostering a culture that celebrates mindfulness and work-life harmony. By advocating for wellness initiatives within his organization, Alex has become a beacon of transformation, demonstrating the possibility of reconciling corporate goals with holistic well-being.

In navigating the intersection of stressful realities and enlightened self-care, Alex's journey champions the narrative of true success—a life where professional aspirations and personal wellness coexist gracefully. His story serves as a compelling testament to the transformative power of stepping back, recalibrating, and embracing balance on the road to a deeply fulfilling life.

As more people seek meaning and balance, stories like Alex's are becoming catalysts for larger shifts—sparking new interest in how we design our homes, cities, and shared spaces.

Review and Implement

Communities are continually evolving, driven by a collective desire for healthier lifestyles, reduced stress, and quality time with family and friends. Recognizing the importance of human connection for health and longevity, there is an increasing emphasis on creating facilities that offer opportunities for self-care and social interaction.[1] An example is Remedy Place in New York City, expanding across the U.S. as a social wellness club.[2] This innovative concept provides a diverse array of self-care options, including AI-enhanced deep tissue massages, in a communal setting.

To support these evolving desires, urban planners and architects are reimagining city, town, and village designs. The integration of AI allows these environments to enhance inhabitants' physical well-being, mental health, and social connections. This leads to the development of mixed-use spaces that blend residential, recreational, and professional areas, promoting a balanced lifestyle amid expanded green spaces. Furthermore, technological advancements like AI-driven services foster community engagement and virtual cultural events, enhancing the sense of belonging. Meanwhile, holistic wellness and sustainable practices are becoming standard features, crafting environments conducive to healthier living for future generations. This approach helps shape living spaces focused on connectivity, creative potential, and well-being, ensuring harmonious communities for all.

According to the Global Wellness Institute (GWI), based in Miami, Florida, the Wellness Real Estate Market is projected to reach $913 billion by 2028.[3] Key current trends influencing this growth include:[4]

Brain-Friendly Buildings: Incorporate neuro-architecture principles—biophilic elements such as green walls, indoor plants, and natural light, circadian lighting that mimics daylight cycles, acoustic design for reduced noise, and tactile finishes—to foster focus and reduce stress.

Smart Wellness Ecosystems: Leverage Artificial Intelligence (AI) and the Internet of Things (IoT) to track air quality, sleep patterns, refrigerated food freshness, and energy use, delivering personalized recommendations—such as automated ventilation adjustments—to optimize health.

Wellness-Centric Mixed-Use Developments: Blend residential, commercial, and recreational spaces—like on-site fitness studios, healthy cafés, and co-working hubs—to create walkable, health-focused communities.

Resilient Tourism and Real Estate: Design climate-adaptive destinations in areas less susceptible to extreme weather, offering global eco-retreats and robust infrastructure that ensures visitor comfort while promoting environmental sustainability.

Bio-Adaptive Living: Incorporate modular, multi-purpose rooms equipped with smart technology and flexible layouts—transforming a living room into a home office or yoga studio—to cater to a tech-savvy generation seeking affordability and functionality.

Respecting Historical and Cultural Contexts: While 20th-century real estate emphasized financial engineering, contemporary developments prioritize collaboration with local stakeholders to preserve and adapt heritage buildings, honoring cultural identity and strengthening community ties.

Great architecture, akin to music, art, and philosophy, serves as an outlet for expressing the human experience during specific historical periods, revealing needs, understandings, and solutions for evolving challenges.

Monitor & Evolve - Sustain Your Growth

Quick Checklist

Finding or Building Wellness Communities

Step 1: Define Community Goals

Define Your Mission:

- **Identify Purpose:** Determine the primary focus of your wellness community (e.g., mindfulness, fitness, holistic health).
- **Set Values:** Establish guiding values for interactions and activities, such as inclusivity, support, and growth.

Step 2: Cultural Sensitivities and Inclusivity

- **Open Invitation:** Design outreach strategies to engage a diverse range of participants.
- **Cultural Sensitivity:** Create a welcoming space for individuals from diverse backgrounds—whether a yoga studio offering multilingual classes,

gender-neutral restrooms, and sliding-scale pricing, or a global franchise adjusting rates to local economies while embracing humility, respect, and openness to noncommercial traditions rich in alternative practices.

- **Inclusive Leadership:** Promote diverse voices in leadership roles to reflect a variety of perspectives and lived experiences.

Step 3: Develop Shared Activities

- **Collaborative Workshops:** Organize events for members to learn from each other and share expertise.
- **Regular Meetups:** Schedule consistent gatherings, both virtual and in-person, to strengthen community bonds.

Step 4: Facilitate Mutual Support

- **Peer Groups:** Form small groups for members to share experiences and provide support.
- **Mentorship Programs:** Create opportunities for experienced members to guide newcomers.

Step 5: Create Communication Channels

- **Open Communication:** Foster dialogue and actively listen to community members' needs and contributions.

- **Feedback Mechanism:** Implement a system for members to offer suggestions and express needs.
- **Encourage Participation:** Provide opportunities for members to lead activities or share feedback.

Online Communities

- **Social Media Groups:** Join Facebook or Instagram groups focused on wellness.
- **Wellness Apps:** Connect through meditation, fitness, or habit-tracking apps with built-in communities.
- **Online Forums:** Engage in specialized discussion boards on health and holistic living.

Offline Communities

- Local Classes and Workshops: Attend yoga studios with soft lighting and calming scents, meditation halls echoing with quiet breath, or fitness classes to connect with peers.
- **Community Centers:** Participate in health talks, support groups, or library-hosted wellness meetups buzzing with conversation.
- **Wellness Retreats:** Immerse yourself in multi-day, dedicated in-person programs for deep personal growth.
- **Educate Yourself:** Learn about the cultural norms and values of community members.

Step 6: Review and Adapt

- **Regular Assessment:** Gather feedback on community effectiveness and identify areas for improvement.
- **Adapt to Change:** Be willing to adjust goals and activities based on member needs and feedback.

The next chapter will guide us into the natural world, revealing how its calming presence enhances holistic health. By understanding nature's role in our well-being, we can foster a more harmonious relationship with our environment, promoting resilience and peace. We'll reconnect and explore how its rhythms can anchor our own—uncovering fresh paths to clarity, connection, and renewal.

CHAPTER 11

NATURE'S ROLE IN HOLISTIC HEALTH

Case Study:

Laura, Environmental Consultant in San Francisco, USA - Escaping to Nature for Solace

Laura, a dedicated environmental consultant in the bustling city of San Francisco, yearned for a deeper connection to nature amidst her demanding career. While her job fulfilled its commitment to sustainability, it often kept her indoors, away from the very environments she sought to protect.

Embracing Nature to Rejuvenate

Recognizing the disconnect between her professional life and personal well-being, Laura consciously decided to immerse herself in activities that bridged this gap. Forest bathing and gardening became her pathways back to nature.

Every weekend, Laura escaped the city's clamor, heading to nearby Redwood National Park for forest bathing. Amidst towering trees and serene silence, she practiced mindfulness, allowing herself to be fully present and absorb the calming aspects of the forest. These moments became vital respites, clearing her mind from the clutter of urban life and work pressures.

Cultivating Balance through Gardening

Back in the city, Laura transformed her small backyard into a lush garden sanctuary. There, she relished the therapeutic benefits of tending to her plants and observing their growth. The satisfaction she derived from nurturing her garden deepened her appreciation for life's interconnectedness, enriching her understanding and sense of fulfillment.

Gardening offered Laura more than just a routine; it became a canvas for creativity and a meditative practice. She carefully selected native plants to nurture, supporting local biodiversity and aligning with her environmental principles. Under her attentive care, the garden flourished, representing the harmonious balance she aspired to achieve personally and professionally.

Integrating Community and Purpose

Immersing herself in nature restored Laura's calm and clarity, strengthening her resilience and giving her a renewed sense of purpose. Motivated by this transformation, she joined local environmental groups to share her experiences and advocate for more urban green spaces. Her leadership sparked community-driven urban gardening projects and park revitalizations, uniting neighbors in celebrating nature's healing power.

Case Study:

Tom, Retired Teacher, Atlanta, USA - Enjoying His Passion for Gardening and Cookery

In Atlanta, Tom, a recently retired high school teacher, embarked on a new chapter centered around his love for gardening and cooking. His career in education had been fulfilling, yet he yearned for the freedom to pursue his passions with the vigor that full-time work scarcely allowed.

Nurturing Growth through Gardening

Tom had long cherished gardening, viewing it as both an art and a science that brought him closer to nature. In retirement, this hobby transformed into a daily ritual of discovery and satisfaction. His backyard, once just a patch of grass, evolved into a vibrant oasis teeming with vegetables and flowers.

Through gardening, Tom found a new rhythm to life. Each morning, he approached the garden with the enthusiasm of an artist beginning a new masterpiece. As he tended to his plants, the physical joy of working the soil and the gratification of watching seeds flourish mirrored the growth and patience he instilled in his students throughout his teaching career.

Culinary Explorations in Cookery

Complementing his passion for gardening was Tom's love for cooking. Retirement afforded him the time to explore culinary arts at leisure, marrying fresh produce from his garden with innovative recipes. The kitchen became his studio, where every meal was an opportunity to experiment with flavors and techniques.

Tom began inviting friends and former colleagues for evening dinners, transforming his home into a hub of social activity. These gatherings showcased his culinary experiments—festivals of taste that brought people together, much like he had united his students in the classroom. The meals nurtured not only his relationships but also shared a piece of his journey, inspiring others to embrace their hobbies fully.

The Joys of a Balanced Life

This immersive engagement with gardening and cooking helped Tom achieve a balance that eluded him during his years of structured schedules and curricular demands. Retirement became not just a cessation of work but a proactive path to personal happiness and community connection.

Through this balance of passions, Tom rediscovered a sense of purpose in fostering growth—whether in his garden or in inspiring others to find fulfillment. His journey highlighted the value of integrating personal interests into daily life, proving that retirement can be a rich tapestry of exploration and joy.

Tom's story illuminates the serenity and satisfaction that come from cultivating one's passions and serves as a reminder of the new adventures and possibilities that await when one embraces each day with enthusiasm and open curiosity.

Like Laura and Tom, we each have the power to deepen our well-being through intentional time in nature. Let's explore how these practices—from ancient traditions to modern tools—can help us reconnect with our roots.

Review and Implement

Nature provides a sanctuary that nurtures and revitalizes our inner selves. Shinrin-yoku, originating in Japan in the 1980s and also known as "forest bathing," involves immersing oneself in the forest atmosphere to promote health and well-being.[1] This practice encourages individuals to engage all their senses in nature, focusing on the sights, sounds, and scents around them. The benefits of Shinrin-yoku are recognized for reducing stress, enhancing mood, and boosting immune function, as the natural environment facilitates relaxation and mindfulness. As urban life grows increasingly hectic, it serves as a valuable retreat to reconnect with nature and nurture mental and physical health. Now practiced worldwide, Shinrin-yoku has become a globally embraced path to restoring inner calm and reducing stress in an increasingly urbanized world. A few key places to visit are listed below.

- Akasawa Natural Recreation Forest, Japan - where it all began[2]
- Caledonian Forest, Scotland [3]
- Costa Rica[4]
- The Morikami Museum and Japanese Gardens, South Florida [5,6]
- The Redwood Forests, California[7]
- Tongass National Forest, Alaska[8]

Gardening, whether tending to a backyard plot or a few pots on a balcony, fosters mental well-being through the rhythm of planting and nurturing life. Hiking opens a path to the physical and mental benefits found in natural settings, allowing us to stride away from tension while embracing serenity. Birdwatching encourages mindfulness through the simple act of observing birds in their natural habitat, while picnics in local parks create moments of relaxation and connection with the open air.

Rooftop landscaping is gaining momentum globally, with countries like China leading the charge by transforming urban rooftops into vibrant green spaces.[9] This movement emphasizes sustainability and environmental consciousness, promoting greener urban environments.

In cities like New York, rooftops are being creatively repurposed by restaurants to grow herbs and vegetables, reflecting an innovative approach to self-sufficiency and fresh produce. Such initiatives contribute to reducing urban heat and improving air quality while offering aesthetic and recreational benefits, creating multi-functional spaces that support healthier lifestyles and community well-being.

Integrating nature into daily life can be transformative. Starting your day with a morning walk in a nearby park or green area sets a tranquil tone that anchors the day. Embrace outdoor lunch breaks for a refreshing change of scenery. Infuse your indoor spaces with greenery; they're not just decorations but lifelines to nature's tranquility. Position your workspace to overlook windows with natural views, inviting the outside in. Finally, plan short weekly trips to local nature spots or gardens. Each visit rekindles your bond with nature and rejuvenates your spirit.

Refine Your Practice - Deepen Your Mastery

Quick Checklist

Five Actionable Ways to Incorporate Nature into Daily Life for Urban Dwellers

Create a Green Space Indoors

- **Indoor Plants & Herbs:** Add potted houseplants or a small herb garden to purify the air and nurture greenery.
- **Natural Decor:** Incorporate stones, shells, driftwood, or wood elements to introduce nature's textures into your décor.

Utilize Public Parks and Green Areas

- **Daily Walks:** Start your day with a walk in a nearby park or green area, or walk during lunch breaks or after work.
- **Lunch Breaks Outdoors:** Take your lunch outside, even if it's on a small patio or balcony.
- **Picnics in Parks:** Spend time in local parks for relaxation and a connection with the open air.
- **Outdoor Exercises:** Practice yoga or tai chi in local green spaces to engage with nature.
- **Forest Bathing:** Immerse yourself in a forest environment to reduce stress and enhance your mood.

Engage in Urban Gardening

- **Gardening:** Planting and tending to a garden can boost mental well-being.
- **Community Gardens:** Join a local community garden project to grow vegetables and flowers.
- **Balcony or Rooftop Gardening:** Transform your balcony or rooftop into a fragrant oasis filled with sun-warmed pots of herbs, climbing vines, and flowers, creating a welcoming green sanctuary.

Incorporate Nature Sounds and Scents

- **Natural Views & Soundtracks:** Position your workspace by a window overlooking greenery and play nature soundtracks—birdsong or waterfalls—to deepen your sense of calm.
- **Essential Oils:** Use diffusers with natural scents like pine and lavender to evoke a forest atmosphere.

Plan Regular Nature Excursions

- **Weekly Nature Outings:** Schedule short weekly trips to local nature spots or gardens.
- **Weekend Getaways:** Plan regular visits to nearby nature reserves or hiking trails.
- **Outdoor Activities:** Organize picnics or bike rides that immerse you in natural settings.
- **Hiking:** Explore local parks to enjoy the outdoors while exercising.

- **Bird Watching:** Observe and listen to birds as a mindful, peaceful activity.

Mental Health Benefits of Nature Immersion

- An article in *Harvard Health* states that spending as little as 20 minutes in nature can significantly reduce cortisol levels].[10]

- A study published in the *International Journal of Environmental Research and Public Health* highlights that exposure to natural environments is associated with reduced levels of depression, anxiety, and stress.[11]

- Research from *Molecular Psychiatry* reveals that an hour spent walking in nature reduces amygdala activation, while the same duration in an urban environment shows stable activation levels. This compelling evidence could influence urban planners to prioritize creating more green spaces, enhancing mental well-being for citizens.[12]

These findings consistently demonstrate that even brief exposure to nature has measurable effects on mental health, making it a simple yet powerful tool in our holistic wellness toolkit.

In the next chapter, we'll explore how sustainable living practices can help us honor the Earth not just in spirit, but through the everyday choices that shape our homes, habits, and hearts.

CHAPTER 12

SUSTAINABLE LIVING FOR HOLISTIC WELL-BEING

Case Study:

Sophie, Interior Designer in Austin, USA - Embracing Sustainability

Sophie, a passionate interior designer in Austin, Texas, sought a deeper connection between her lifestyle and the planet's health. Already on a mission to live more eco-consciously, she felt overwhelmed about where to begin making substantial changes. However, an enlightening moment at a local community sustainability fair sparked her transformation and set her on a dedicated path toward sustainable living.

The Catalyst for Change

At the fair, Sophie was captivated by the innovation and simplicity of sustainable practices, which emphasized how small changes could lead to significant impacts. This revelation inspired her to embark on her eco-journey, integrating sustainable principles into her daily life and work. With each small change, from reducing waste to mindfully selecting materials for her designs, Sophie not only decreased her environmental footprint but also significantly enhanced her well-being.

Practical and Sustainable Transformations

One of Sophie's first steps was exploring zero-waste basics by assessing her personal waste production. She introduced reusable items into her routine—cloth bags, stainless steel water bottles, and glass containers—ensuring these essentials became staples in her daily activities. Sophie also embraced composting, transforming kitchen scraps into rich soil for a community garden she helped nurture.

Through her work, Sophie adopted sustainable design practices, opting for recycled materials and energy-efficient solutions. Her projects reflected her commitment to sustainability while educating her clients on the benefits of eco-friendly living. This approach brought new depth to her personal and professional life, intertwining her vocation with her values.

Sophie's Inspiration Coupled with an Introduction to Feng Shui

Sophie discovered that clearing clutter and embracing clean, open designs provided her with newfound mental clarity and calm, aligning perfectly with her belief that spaces should nurture well-being. To extend this benefit to her clients, she partnered with a Feng Shui consultant to arrange rooms for optimal energy flow and harmony. By applying these principles, her designs became both uplifting and beautiful, enhancing mood and functionality. Inspired by the impact on her own life and her clients', Sophie trained as a Feng Shui Practitioner. Her expertise quickly drew attention, transforming both residential and commercial spaces and propelling her business to new heights.

Feng Shui Principles

Feng Shui, literally meaning "wind" and "water," has roots tracing back thousands of years to the early Zhou dynasty in China. It is closely linked to astronomy and the natural environment, focusing on harmonizing the human experience by understanding the flow of Qi, or vital life energy, which courses through landscapes, impacting health and prosperity. (Kensa, the Japanese equivalent, similarly emphasizes spatial harmony and energy flow rooted in aesthetic simplicity.)1

Origins and Philosophy

- **Taoist Philosophy:** Feng Shui is deeply embedded in Taoist thought, focusing on the natural balance between humans and their environment.

- **Yin and Yang:** These represent harmonious forces essential for maintaining balance within a space.

- **The Five Elements:** The interaction of Wood, Fire, Earth, Metal, and Water plays a crucial role. Each element has unique attributes and relationships that create and destroy, influencing energy flow. Properly balanced, they enhance prosperity and health.

- **Wood:** Associated with growth and creativity.

- **Fire:** Linked to passion and vitality.

- **Earth:** Represents stability and nourishment.

- **Metal:** Symbolizes clarity and precision.

- **Water:** Conveys fluidity and adaptability.

With these core principles in mind, the next step is learning how to translate this energetic philosophy into everyday spatial design using one of Feng Shui's most important tools, the Bagua Map.

The Bagua Map

The Bagua Map is an essential tool in Feng Shui, serving as a blueprint to align spaces with specific life aspects such as family, wealth, and health. The Bagua, literally meaning "eight symbols," is an octagonal chart divided into nine segments, each corresponding to different dimensions of life like career, relationships, and personal growth.

To use it, align the bottom row of the map (career area) with the wall that contains the main entrance to the space—this helps you assess which areas of your home correspond to specific life areas.

Detailed Breakdown of the Bagua Map

- **Wealth and Prosperity (*Xun*)** - Positioned in the southeast corner of the Bagua, this area governs abundance and financial success. Enhancements often involve elements that signify wind and wood, like plants or flowing water.

- **Fame and Reputation (*Li*)** - Located in the south, this section relates to how one is perceived within a community. Incorporating fire elements such as candles or red colors can invigorate this space.

- **Love and Relationships (*Kun*)** - Situated in the southwest, focusing on this area can foster romantic relationships and partnerships. Elements like pink colors and paired objects encourage harmony here.

- **Family and Health (*Zhen*)** - In the east, this segment influences familial connections and well-being. Incorporating wood elements, such as flowers or wooden furniture, can amplify nurturing energy.

- **Health and Unity (*Tai Qi*)** - Central to the Bagua, this area governs overall wellness and unity. Maintaining a clutter-free and open space here promotes positive energy flow throughout the home.
- **Children and Creativity (*Dui*)** - This sector, located in the west, fosters generative ideas and new beginnings. Metal elements, such as frames or sculptures, stimulate creative endeavors.
- **Knowledge and Self-Cultivation (*Gen*)** - Situated in the northeast, this area encourages intellectual growth and personal development. Earth elements like stones or books enhance learning opportunities.
- **Career and Life Path (*Kan*)** - Positioned in the north, this sector signifies direction and career prospects. Water features and the color black improve focus in this realm.
- **Helpful People and Travel (*Qian*)** - Found in the northwest, this area relates to support networks and travel potential. Metal items and colors like gray or white optimize this sector.

Utilizing the Bagua Map in Spaces

In practice, a certified Feng Shui consultant uses the Bagua map alongside tools like the Luo Pan compass to assess a space. By analyzing how different areas align with the nine Bagua sectors, they recommend alterations—such as rearranging furniture, introducing specific elements, or adjusting color schemes—to harmonize energies and enhance various aspects of life. This methodology underpins Feng Shui's goal of creating balanced and prosperous environments that promote holistic well-being. By addressing each of these segments, Feng Shui practitioners optimize the flow of Qi to enhance overall harmony in living and working spaces.

The Luo Shu Magic Square and the Bagua Map

The Luo Shu Magic Square is an ancient symbol deeply rooted in Chinese legend, dating back to 2800 B.C. It is particularly noted for its mathematical and cultural significance. This mystical symbol emerged during a time of distress when a great flood afflicted ancient China, believed to have angered the river god, *Luo*. To appease the deity, the people made sacrificial offerings, at which point a turtle reportedly appeared from the river, bearing the Luo Shu pattern on its shell.

The Legend of the Luo Shu Turtle

Legend has it that the turtle's shell features a nine-grid magic square, with each row, column, and diagonal summing to 15—a number reflecting the 15-day span of each of the 24 solar cycles. This cosmic symmetry, symbolizing harmony among heaven, earth, and humanity, was believed to grant mystical powers, guiding river management and other natural forces.

Cultural and Symbolic Significance

In ancient Chinese culture, the Luo Shu Magic Square was revered not merely as a mathematical curiosity but as a divine guide for understanding and mastering the balance of natural elements. It symbolized the harmonious flows of energy, crucial to practices like Feng Shui, where these energies are directed to create balance and prosperity in environments.

This legendary square is mentioned in "The Book of Rites," a canonical Chinese text documenting cultural practices and legends, including another tale about a dragon rising from the Yellow River with the Ho Tu, or Yellow River Map, on its scales. Both stories emphasize the ancient Chinese belief in the connection between cosmological structures and earthly control.

Though centuries have passed, the Luo Shu Magic Square remains influential in Chinese philosophy and modern applications, particularly in Feng Shui, where its principles help map the energetic and physical structure of spaces.

Broader Cultural Usage

The concept of magic squares similar to the Luo Shu also appears in other ancient civilizations, including Persia, Arabia, India, and Babylon.[2] Across these cultures, they served various roles, from rituals and astrology to amulets, signifying their universal appeal and application as a bridge between the earth and the celestial. Additionally, they are instrumental in teaching modern matrix operations and understanding determinants due to their orderly structure. They enhance comprehension of broader mathematical themes in combinatorics and number theory, providing a foundational gateway to investigate numerical patterns and their diverse applications.

The Luo Pan Compass[3]

- **Circular Design**: The Luo Pan consists of a circular wooden base, rich in detail, with multiple concentric rings. These rings are inscribed with Chinese characters, symbols, and specific Feng Shui formulas. They include the eight trigrams from the I Ching and other elements like the Heavenly Stems and Earthly Branches, the 24 directions known as the "mountains," and constellations.

- **Central Magnetic Needle**: Unlike a standard compass, the Luo Pan's needle interacts with several symbolic rings to help Feng Shui practitioners read the energetic flow of a space and align it with natural forces and cosmic patterns.

Functional Roles

- **Determining Orientation**: One of the primary uses of the Luo Pan is to ascertain the most favorable directional alignments for buildings and rooms. Feng Shui experts rely on this compass to ensure spaces are arranged coherently with both their immediate environment and celestial influences to optimize the flow of Qi.

- **Geomantic Readings**: The compass is used for more than just geographic direction. It enables practitioners to interpret how temporal forces, topographical features, and elemental energies interact, which is essential for balancing and harmonizing living spaces with cosmic forces.

Symbolism and Cultural Heritage

- **Emblem of Knowledge**: The Luo Pan embodies a wealth of traditional Chinese knowledge, serving as a synthesis of the natural, spiritual, and physical world elements that promote balanced and prosperous settings.

- **Cultural Significance**: This instrument is a cornerstone of Chinese tradition. It reflects ancient philosophical ideas that view landscapes and spatial arrangements as linked to fortune and fate, highlighting its integral role in cultural heritage practices.

Modern Applications

Today, the Luo Pan remains an indispensable tool for certified Feng Shui consultants who incorporate it into modern design and architecture. It aids in creating harmonious environments in both residential and commercial settings worldwide, marrying age-old metaphysical insights with contemporary architectural needs. By ensuring aligned spatial organization, the Luo Pan continues to be a valuable asset for those seeking enhanced living conditions through a blend of practical wisdom and philosophical understanding.

Historical Context and Impact

Feng Shui historically guided architectural and urban planning in China, influencing the siting of emperors' palaces and burial grounds to harness favorable invisible forces. Its long-standing cultural validation suggests its practical utility in achieving balanced living spaces, though scientific proof varies.

Modern Applications and Methodologies

Today, Feng Shui principles transcend cultural boundaries, influencing both residential and commercial design globally.

- **Relationship Benefits**: Adopting Feng Shui can enhance mental clarity and reduce stress, improving overall quality of life. It fosters better relationship dynamics by harmonizing personal spaces, promoting a blend of traditional wisdom and modern lifestyle desires.

- **Residential Harmony**: Strategic placements ensure balanced Qi flow, promoting health and happiness.

- **Corporate Spaces**: Feng Shui is utilized to increase productivity and satisfaction in the workplace. It considers desk positioning, color schemes, and lighting to foster creativity and minimize stress.

- **Certified Practitioners**: Using tools like the Bagua map and Luo Pan compass, they assess energy distribution and propose specific enhancements, such as furniture repositioning or element integration, to boost energy flow; they tailor interventions to individual needs, enhancing specific life aspects.

- **Global Influence**: Spanning architecture, design, and urban planning, Feng Shui enhances workspaces, hospitality, healthcare, and branding by aligning environments with human needs for greater health, productivity, and well-being.

By blending traditional wisdom with modern lifestyles, Feng Shui promotes clearer thinking, reduced tension, and a deeper sense of well-being, reflecting its enduring global appeal.

Case Study:

Carlos, Architect in São Paulo, Brazil - Advocate for Sustainable Living

In São Paulo, Brazil, Carlos, an innovative architect, embarked on a journey of sustainable living, aiming to blend his professional skills with personal wellness. Passionate about minimizing environmental impact, Carlos sought to integrate eco-friendly practices into both his designs and daily life.

Catalyst for Change: An Eco-Conscious Design Conference

An eye-opening experience at an international eco-design conference became the catalyst for Carlos's transformation. Inspired by the innovative use of sustainable materials and energy-efficient designs showcased, he returned to São Paulo determined to enact impactful changes, starting with his own lifestyle.

Carlos implemented sustainable practices in his architecture firm, incorporating recycled materials, green roofs, and passive solar design into his blueprints. These changes not only enhanced the environmental efficiency of his projects but also inspired his colleagues and clients to embrace sustainability in their endeavors.

Integrating Sustainability into Daily Life

At home, Carlos adopted a minimalist lifestyle focused on reducing waste and conserving resources. He switched to energy-efficient appliances and embraced a zero-waste mindset. Each small choice contributed to a holistic lifestyle prioritizing balance and mindfulness.

Carlos also cultivated a transformative rooftop garden, utilizing urban space to grow organic vegetables and herbs. This city oasis became a refuge, providing fresh produce and a daily reminder of the beauty and benefits of sustainable living. Cooking with ingredients he nurtured deepened his connection to nature and offered a sense of accomplishment.

Fostering Community and Environmental Awareness

Carlos's passion for sustainable living extended to his community involvement. He began hosting workshops to educate local residents and businesses about sustainable practices, from energy conservation to urban gardening. His efforts galvanized a movement within the neighborhood, inspiring community gardens and collaborative environmental projects.

Through these actions, Carlos demonstrated that sustainable living transcends personal wellness, fostering community resilience and encouraging collective environmental responsibility. His story reflects the impact of aligning professional expertise with a commitment to sustainability, creating a ripple effect that inspires broader change.

Growing Sustainable Design Awareness in Brazil

In Brazil, awareness of sustainable design is rising across residential, commercial, and community initiatives, reflecting a nationwide commitment to environmental consciousness. Architects, planners, governments, and NGOs are collaborating to integrate green building practices, energy-efficient technologies, and natural elements—such as green roofs, urban gardens, and renewable energy—into eco-friendly infrastructure. Supported by forward-thinking policies, this movement is transforming Brazilian cities into healthier, more cohesive communities and championing ecological stewardship for future generations.[4,5,6]

Favelas

In Brazil, the awareness and implementation of sustainable design are transforming favelas, urban settlements traditionally known for dense populations and inadequate infrastructure. As part of a broader movement toward environmental consciousness, these areas are being reimagined as green spaces, benefiting both residents and the environment.

Urban planners are introducing projects that emphasize waste reduction, efficient water use, and improved air quality. By fostering community engagement and participation, these initiatives empower residents to actively transform their surroundings into sustainable environments. Through education and collaboration, these projects promote ownership and pride, enabling residents to maintain and expand on green initiatives.

Visionary: Ester Carro

Ester Carro, a visionary architect in her mid-20s, recently embarked on an ambitious dream to revolutionize a neglected area within the Jardim Colombo favela on the outskirts of Sao Paulo, the very neighborhood where she spent her formative years.[7] Once a small farm with grazing cows and horses, the area had deteriorated into a hazardous landfill as its original owner became too ill to maintain it. The site, overwhelmed by heaps of refuse and infested with snakes and scorpions, emitted methane fumes from decomposing waste—posing a significant environmental and health risk to the community. Effective waste management was often hindered in favela communities due to challenging topography, flooding, and lack of proper infrastructure.

Despite ascending to a role within the mayor's office, Ester remained deeply connected to her roots and committed to sparking change. Her early inspiration came from accompanying her father, a former construction worker who became a community leader, to various project sites within the community. These experiences, coupled with learning about the transformation of a trash dump in Rio de Janeiro's Vidigal favela into the ecological reserve Parque Ecologico Sitiê, fueled her determination to create Fazendinhando Park.[8]

Eager to reimagine the landfill as a community oasis, Ester recruited volunteers to help remove tons of garbage by hand over two arduous years. With little backing from local authorities and skepticism from the community, she relied on her creativity and perseverance to galvanize support and share her vision for a public green space.

Once the debris was cleared, Ester and the volunteers scoured the neighborhood for discarded materials to repurpose in the park. Discarded car tires became vibrant seating, and an old refrigerator found new life as a lending library. Next, Ester enlisted 40 graffiti artists to cover the walls with colorful murals, gradually transforming the park into a cultural and artistic hub. Looking toward the future, her vision includes developing a community vegetable garden and adding a gazebo for concerts, further strengthening community bonds and eco-consciousness.

While Ester plans to extend her expertise to other favela communities across Brazil, Fazendinhando Park remains a deeply personal project. Her story offers inspiration for struggling inner-city areas worldwide. Importantly, these projects focus on educating future generations through hands-on experiences, equipping them with skills to use and pass on. Volunteering further extends to youth education and childcare services, enabling parents to work and fostering pride through artistic expression. By instilling hope and unleashing creativity, these efforts offer one of the greatest gifts to communities worldwide.

Visionary: Gabriel Kozlowski

Gabriel Kozlowski is a distinguished Brazilian architect and curator whose innovative contributions have significantly enriched both Brazilian and global architecture. His academic journey, rooted in theoretical and practical expertise, laid the groundwork for his pioneering work in the field. His influence stretches to esteemed events like the 17th International Architecture Exhibition in Venice, where he served as an assistant curator in 2021. He also curated influential exhibitions such as "Walls of Air" at the 2018 Venice Architecture Biennale and "Housing+" at MIT's Center for Advanced Urbanism.[9,10,11]

Throughout his illustrious career, Gabriel has authored influential texts, including "The World as an Architectural Project", and "8 Reactions for Afterwards," discussing eight key territory transformations: Demarcate, Colonize, Evoke, Crack, Stake, Replicate, Tie, and Mask". He held notable positions at the Massachusetts Institute of Technology, contributing to the School of Architecture and Planning, the Center for Advanced Urbanism, and the SENSEable

City Lab. Now pursuing his PhD at Harvard Graduate School of Design, he serves as the principal of the architectural firm POLES – Political Ecology of Space, with offices in Rio de Janeiro and Boston.[12,13,14]

Gabriel's vision for the future of architecture champions the seamless integration of ecological responsibility with human-centric design. His projects emphasize sustainability, creating spaces that enhance human experience while maintaining ecological balance. Raised amidst Brazil's rich cultural and architectural heritage, his designs marry traditional and contemporary techniques, transforming urban landscapes into inclusive and functional community areas.

The crux of Gabriel's philosophy is adaptive design that melds technology with nature, producing environments that are as visually captivating as they are environmentally sustainable. He envisions a future where urban design extends its role beyond aesthetics to actively enhance individual well-being and quality of life, preserving the planet for future generations. Through his visionary projects and academic contributions, Gabriel continues to inspire the architectural community, illustrating the impact of thoughtful design in forging a more sustainable and harmonious world.

Visual Data Maps

Through his groundbreaking projects, such as "Walls of Air," Gabriel uses visual data maps to illuminate urbanization patterns while highlighting broader societal walls and barriers—both physical and ideological—that hinder Brazil's progress toward a more egalitarian society. The mapping serves as a powerful tool to reveal spatial and political decisions typically hidden, enabling a critical examination of these decisions. This visibility acts as the initial step toward addressing underlying problems, acknowledging their existence to facilitate corrective action.

By drawing on Brazil's context, he collaborates with global thought leaders from various disciplines to rethink architecture's role in societal advancement, reimagine and improve urban design, and challenge existing norms to foster a more egalitarian society.

- The spatial consequences and physical imprints left on Brazilian territories in recent decades include:
- The impact of political borders on Brazil's economic landscapes.
- Interactions between human and natural ecosystems.
- The flow of people due to immigration.
- The movement of commodities and materials.
- The specialization of capital across different national regions.

By mapping Brazil's humidity patterns, Gabriel reveals a significant flow from the Amazon Forest towards the southeast, emphasizing the vital role these natural pathways play for urban areas reliant on northern regions. Choices around deforestation, which release substantial carbon emissions, have far-reaching global consequences due to the Amazon's crucial role in climate stability. This interconnectedness is vividly illustrated by recent droughts and temperature spikes that transform São Paulo's day into an eerie night, reminiscent of California's experience with wildfire smoke. Through impactful visual map illustrations, the global reach of local decisions becomes undeniable, showing how actions taken within one region can ripple across the world, affecting environments and populations worldwide.

Mapping Brazil's political boundaries also uncovers the complex routes roads take to navigate natural features like mountains and rivers, highlighting challenges faced in border regions. Gabriel emphasizes that societies can often become prisoners of their circumstances, while indigenous communities, in contrast, operate without such borders.

He underscores the urgent need for new solidarity and solutions, supported by initiatives like "Tomorrow Anew," which collaborates with NGOs to assist vulnerable populations in São Paulo's slums and those affected by the pandemic in the US and Kenya. This effort stresses the importance of addressing critical issues to drive societal progress and equity, advocating for sustainable global development and unity.

Review and Implement

Sustainable living is not a distant ideal; it's a joyful, fulfilling lifestyle that benefits the planet while enhancing mental clarity, emotional peace, and daily purpose.

Reflect & Celebrate - Honor Your Journey

Quick Checklist

Starter Guide for Transitioning to Sustainable Practices

1. Zero-Waste Basics:

- Evaluate your personal waste production to identify areas for reduction.
- Integrate reusable items such as water bottles, cloth bags, and containers into your daily routine.
- Compost kitchen scraps to decrease food waste and enrich soil in your garden.

2. Energy Conservation:

- Optimize lighting and appliances: switch to LED bulbs, use energy-efficient devices, and maximize natural daylight.
- Unplug electronics when not in use to reduce energy consumption.

3. Sustainable Shopping:

- Choose locally sourced and seasonal produce to support local farmers and reduce transport emissions.
- Select products with minimal packaging to decrease waste.
- Support sustainability-focused brands to encourage ethical production practices.

4. Feng Shui-Inspired Simplicity:

- Declutter and minimize belongings to create open spaces that enhance qi flow.
- Incorporate natural elements like wood or plants to invite balance and health.
- Position furniture to encourage free movement and harmonious energy, creating a balanced and nourishing environment.
- Use calming colors aligned with the Bagua map to invigorate specific areas of your life, promoting a holistic and sustainable lifestyle.

Addressing Misconceptions About Sustainability

- **Time-Consuming**: Sustainable changes can often be simple swaps or habits integrated into existing routines, saving time in the long run (e.g., meal prepping reduces daily cooking time).

- **Expensive**: Initial investments (like reusable products) can lead to long-term savings. Many sustainable practices, such as reducing energy use, actually cut costs.

7-Day Sustainable Habits and Feng Shui Challenge

Day 1: Reduce Single-Use Plastics

- Carry a reusable bag, water bottle, and coffee cup.
- Avoid using any single-use plastic items today.
- Declutter your living space of single-use plastics; ensure that the entrance of your home is clear of clutter to invite positive energy.

Day 2: Energy Conservation

- Turn off lights and unplug devices when not in use.
- Take short showers to reduce water wastage.
- Open windows for natural light and fresh air, which refresh stagnant energy and improve qi flow.

Day 3: Embrace Public or Active Transport

- Walk, bike, or use public transport instead of driving, even for one trip to start.
- Arrange your furniture to facilitate easy movement within your space, promoting a smooth flow of energy.

Day 4: Sustainable Eating

- Plan meals using a weekly menu to minimize waste.
- Prepare a plant-based meal using local produce.
- Focus on reducing meat consumption and supporting local farmers.
- Create a dining setting that encourages relaxation and conversation, perhaps by using circular tables or arrangements symbolizing unity and community.

Day 5: Waste Reduction

- Declutter responsibly by donating unused items.
- Implement a "no waste" day; compost food scraps and recycle effectively.
- Generate as little waste as possible.
- Participate in or organize a community clean-up, reconnecting with and giving back to your environment.
- Clear out items that no longer serve a purpose to enhance the flow of new opportunities and fresh energy into your life.

Day 6: Eco-Friendly Products

- Switch to eco-friendly household and personal care products.
- Identify and use sustainable alternatives for daily items.

- Replace single-use items with reusable alternatives.
- Incorporate natural elements like plants or stones in your home to enhance balance and invoke tranquility.

Day 7: Nature Connection

- Spend time in nature and reflect on personal sustainability goals.
- Make a plan to continue integrating sustainable habits into daily life.
- Arrange a specific area in your home to reflect nature's presence, incorporating elements like wood, metal, or water to maintain a connection with the earth.

In the next chapter, we will explore the role spirituality plays in holistic health, how it enriches every aspect of our lives, and provides a deeper sense of purpose and connection. Prepare to embark on a journey that uncovers the core spiritual elements within holistic well-being, allowing for an elevated, harmonious existence.

CHAPTER 13

SPIRITUALITY AS A CORE OF HOLISTIC HEALTH

Case Study:

Alejandro, Department Head, Global NGO in Washington, D.C., USA - A Spiritual Awakening

In the bustling hub of Washington, D.C., Alejandro held a prominent role at a global NGO, where he dedicated his career to funding opportunities for young entrepreneurs across South America. Despite his professional accomplishments, Alejandro felt a spiritual void, a yearning to connect more deeply with himself and the universe beyond the confines of his busy life.

The Call of the Andes: A Pilgrimage Along the Inca Trail to Machu Picchu

Answering this call for spiritual rejuvenation, Alejandro embarked on an inspiring pilgrimage along the Inca Trail to Machu Picchu, Peru. This adventure offered him a much-needed retreat from the demands of his corporate life and into a realm rich with historical and spiritual significance. The awe-inspiring views from the ancient city of Machu Picchu, cradled by majestic Andean peaks, evoked profound emotions within him.

The trek, spanning four days and covering paths once traversed by the Incas, stretched from the Sacred Valley to Machu Picchu, an emblematic symbol of Incan civilization. Hikers, including Alejandro, walked approximately six hours a day, camping along the trail. Their first night was spent under the stars at Wayllabamba, almost 11,000 feet high, where despite the lack of showers or hot water, the magnificent mountain views made everything worthwhile.

As the journey continued, they camped at Phuyapatamarca and Wiñay Wayna, sites perched over 12,000 feet up and close to Machu Picchu. These campsites offered a deep connection to the Andean land, immersing Alejandro and fellow travelers in nature's wild beauty and the serenity it provides.

Throughout the pilgrimage, skilled Cusco tour guides enriched the experience by sharing fascinating legends and myths of the Inca Empire, highlighting architectural marvels along the way. Communal meals with like-minded hikers added to the sense of camaraderie and were seen as outstanding cultural exchanges.

Guided by local spiritual leaders, Alejandro engaged in traditional ceremonial practices that deepened his connection with the earth and cosmos. Sunrise ceremonies at the revered Sun Gate became pivotal moments of reflection, as the first light not only illuminated the ancient stones but also sparked introspective revelations within him.

Alejandro's pilgrimage was more than a physical challenge; it was a sacred journey to rediscover the spirituality and rich cultural tapestry of the Andean region, connecting with both history and the transformative potential of nature.

Enlightening Experiences: Integration of the Spiritual Journey

His experience at Machu Picchu marked a turning point in Alejandro's life. With newfound clarity and purpose, he returned to his role in Washington, D.C., committed to infusing his daily routine with spiritual practices. Embracing meditation and mindful breathing exercises became his daily rituals, enhancing his resilience and focus amidst the pressures of his high-profile position.

At work, Alejandro began weaving spiritual principles into his team's operations. By introducing mindfulness initiatives and workshops, he fostered a workplace culture centered on compassion, innovation, and holistic growth. These initiatives not only inspired his colleagues but also reinforced the organization's ethos of community empowerment and sustainable development.

So inspired by his journey, Alejandro began researching other ancient sites worldwide, particularly those aligning with solstice and equinox sunsets and key stellar constellations. He compiled a shortlist of places to visit in the future, including:

1. Nazca Lines, Peru]: Discovered in the 1940s and located southeast of Lima, the Nazca Lines consist of geoglyphs depicting plants, animals, and humanoids. Many align with the sun during solstices and equinoxes, indicating the ancient Nazca culture's advanced understanding of celestial events.[3]

2. Newgrange, Ireland: Situated 26 miles north of Dublin, Newgrange is a massive circular structure around 5,000 years old, predating Stonehenge and the Pyramids. Known for its alignment with the winter solstice, it showcases the ancient Europeans' understanding of solar cycles.[4]

3. Temple of Karnak, Egypt: In Luxor, the Temple of Karnak was built over 4,000 years ago and dedicated to Amun-Ra, the sun god, reflecting ancient Egyptian solar worship.[5]

4. Ancient Tomb, Qubbet el-Hawa, Egypt: Built around 1830 BC, light hits the tomb's rear on the winter solstice, highlighting the Egyptians' advanced knowledge of celestial events.[6]

5. Pueblo Bonito, New Mexico, US: Constructed by the Puebloans between 850 and 1150, this large house in Chaco Canyon aligns with astronomical landmarks. Light shines through two second-story windows on the south face for just eight weeks leading up to the winter solstice, suggesting a sophisticated understanding of solar heating.[7]

6. Chichen Itza, Mexico: El Castillo, or the Pyramid of Kukulkan (the feathered serpent god), exemplifies the Mayans' advanced architectural and astronomical knowledge. During both spring and fall equinoxes, a shadow resembling a serpent slides down the side of the Pyramid as the sun sets.[8]

7. Mnajdra Temples, Malta: Among Malta's seven megalithic temples, Mnajdra stands out for its apparent alignment with the summer and winter solstices. While some archaeologists believe this alignment is intentional, others suggest it may be coincidental—further studies continue to explore whether early Maltese builders tracked celestial movements by design or by chance.[9]

8. Stonehenge, England: This iconic site draws crowds to witness the sun setting in alignment with the stones during the winter solstice. Although its exact purpose remains unknown, it likely served as a gathering place for celebrating celestial and societal events simultaneous with winter solstice feasts. Nearby is **Woodhenge**, a bustling hub before Stonehenge's stone phase, where celebratory feasts occurred, marked by alignments for solstices, with processions traditionally connecting to Stonehenge.[10,,11]

9. Nabta Playa, Egypt: Built over 7,000 years ago by cattle-herding nomads some 700 miles south of the Great Pyramid of Giza, Nabta Playa is the world's oldest stone circle. Its stones align precisely with the summer solstice and the onset of monsoon rains, revealing a sophisticated grasp of celestial cycles that guided both ritual life and early calendrical systems. Other markers within the circle target the rising points of Sirius and the constellation Orion, suggesting it is the Earth's oldest astronomical observatory.[12]

These sites represent more than human ingenuity—they illustrate how our ancestors viewed the sun and stars as timeless symbols of guidance, clarity, and rebirth. The reliable dawn of the sun offered daily renewal, while constellations served as celestial guides through the night, weaving cosmic cycles into spiritual practices across cultures.

Ongoing Impact: A Life Recalibrated

Alejandro's story serves as an example for others in high-pressure careers, demonstrating that spiritual exploration is a vital element of holistic well-being, capable of fostering personal growth and meaningful impact both within and beyond the workplace. His transformation at Machu Picchu wasn't fleeting—it sparked a lasting commitment to carve out space in his life for silence, intention, and inner alignment, which influenced his leadership style and deepened his connection with colleagues and causes he championed.

Machu Picchu

Machu Picchu, a UNESCO World Heritage site and one of the Seven New Wonders of the World, stands as an iconic symbol of ancient Inca civilization, located high in the Andes Mountains of Peru at about 2,430 meters above sea level. This 15th-century citadel, often referred to as the "Lost City of the Incas," was constructed during the reign of Inca emperor Pachacuti around 1450, although it was abandoned a century later during the Spanish conquest.

Architectural and Cultural Significance

- **Construction and Layout:** Machu Picchu is renowned for its finely crafted stonework using a technique called ashlar, where stones are cut to fit together without mortar. The site is divided into agricultural, urban, and religious sectors, demonstrating sophisticated planning and agricultural innovation with terraces that allowed for diverse crops.

- **Astrological Importance:** Many aspects of Machu Picchu align with astronomical events, reflecting the Incas' advanced understanding of cosmology. Structures like the Intihuatana stone were used as an astronomical clock or calendar, emphasizing the significant role the heavens played in Inca culture.

Historical Discovery

- **Rediscovery:** Although known to locals, Machu Picchu escaped the attention of Spanish conquistadors. It remained unknown to the outside world until American historian Hiram Bingham brought it to international attention in 1911. This discovery sparked global interest in Inca culture and history, making Machu Picchu a world-renowned archaeological site.

Modern Importance

- **Tourist Attraction:** As one of the most visited sites in Peru, Machu Picchu attracts millions of tourists annually. Its stunning location, combined with the mystery surrounding its original purpose—whether as a royal estate, religious site, or military stronghold—continues to captivate visitors and scholars.
- **Conservation Efforts:** The site faces challenges due to its popularity and environmental impacts,

necessitating ongoing conservation efforts to preserve its structural integrity and cultural significance.

Today, Machu Picchu remains not only an extraordinary relic of Inca engineering and architectural excellence but also an emblem of cultural heritage and human achievement, inspiring countless stories and research about its enigmatic past.

Case Study:

Javier, International Scholar in Barcelona, Spain - A Spiritual Pilgrimage to El Camino de Santiago

Living amidst the vibrant culture of Barcelona, Spain, Javier, an internationally respected scholar specializing in global finance, found himself deeply inquisitive about the world's spiritual diversity. Known for his analytical acumen, Javier's career engaged him in financial discussions across countries, yet he felt a growing need to explore the spiritual commonalities connecting different cultures—a curiosity he had long nurtured.

A Journey of Spiritual Exploration

Javier had long aspired to walk the Camino de Santiago, captivated by its spiritual depth and historical significance.13 More than an adventure, he viewed this journey as a chance to connect deeply with his spiritual self and explore diverse global faith practices along the way.

Preparation

Understanding the physical and mental demands of the Camino Frances, Javier rigorously prepared for the journey. Over several months, he incorporated daily walking and strength training, complementing his regimen with meditation and yoga to enhance his spiritual focus. He carefully curated his gear—lightweight clothing, sturdy boots, and a minimalist backpack—to align with the Camino's ethos of simplicity and resilience.

The Journey Begins

As Javier embarked on his pilgrimage across the picturesque landscapes of northern Spain, each stage offered profound introspection. Interacting with fellow pilgrims from diverse backgrounds enriched his understanding of spirituality's global tapestry and deepened his appreciation for how these practices connect communities worldwide.

Challenges and Revelations

Navigating the Camino Frances, whether crossing the Pyrenees or walking through the serene forests of Galicia, presented Javier with both physical challenges and spiritual insights. Each step brought clarity and perspective, aligning him with the historic and spiritual traditions embedded in the trail.

Culmination and Integration

Upon reaching the Cathedral of Santiago de Compostela, Javier experienced a profound transformation, witnessing the powerful convergence of faith and humanity. This change extended beyond the Camino, as he integrated spiritual practices into his academic life in Barcelona. He infused meditation and ethical considerations into his financial teachings, enhancing both personal and professional growth.

Promoting Spiritual Connection

Inspired by his transformation, Javier began championing spiritual discussions within his academic circle, initiating dialogues that bridge spirituality and global issues. Through seminars and workshops, he highlighted how spiritual values nurture interconnected global communities.

Javier's journey was more than a pilgrimage; it was a testament to spirituality's pivotal role in holistic health, advancing personal growth and a broader understanding of global unity.

Camino Frances - El Camino de Santiago

The Camino Frances, or "The French Way," is the most popular and historic route on the *El Camino de Santiago*, a network of pilgrimages leading to the shrine of the apostle St. James in the Cathedral of Santiago de Compostela in Spain. Known for its rich history and cultural significance, the Camino Frances stretches approximately 780 kilometers from St. Jean Pied de Port in France, across the Pyrenees, through Spain's picturesque landscapes, to its final destination at Santiago de Compostela.[14]

Historical and Cultural Significance

- **Origins**: The roots of the Camino trace back to the Middle Ages, serving as a spiritual journey for pilgrims seeking penance and growth. Over the centuries, it has evolved into a path of personal discovery, reflection, and community.

- **Cultural Diversity**: The route passes through diverse regions of Spain, each contributing unique cultural influences, cuisine, and traditions. Pilgrims experience a mosaic of architectural styles, historic landmarks, and rich folklore that define the northern Spanish landscape.

Pilgrimage Experience

- **Spiritual Journey**: Walking the Camino Frances is often seen as a way to reconnect with oneself and nature, providing both physical challenges and spiritual enrichment. The route fosters introspection, promoting a deep sense of connection with fellow travelers from around the world.

- **Hospitality and Tradition**: Pilgrims find shelter in *albergues* (hostels) along the route, where they experience the renowned hospitality of the Camino. Despite modern amenities, traces of the ancient pilgrimage remain, resonating with those who walk this historic path.

The Concluding Pilgrimage

For many, reaching Santiago de Compostela signifies the fulfillment of a transformative journey. The completion at the cathedral, a masterpiece of Gothic and Baroque architecture, serves as a powerful symbol of devotion and personal achievement. The Camino Frances holds a special place in the hearts of those who undertake it, illustrating a timeless blend of historical legacy and personal introspection.

Like Alejandro's path, Javier's journey reveals that spiritual discovery is deeply personal yet universally resonant. While their paths differed in culture and form, their transformations echo a universal truth: spiritual growth isn't bound by any one tradition; it thrives where intention, humility, and presence converge. Let's now explore how you can reflect on and strengthen your own spiritual connection.

Review and Implement

Spirituality isn't limited to any single belief system—it's a universal human experience that invites empathy, connection, and inner peace. Whether grounded in faith traditions or personal reflection, everyone has a path to explore.

Envision the Future - Step Boldly Forward

Quick Checklist

Here's a reflective journal prompt to guide you: Take a moment to ponder your core spiritual beliefs. How do they support or shape your approach to balancing mind, body, and spirit? Use this reflection to identify insights or actions you can integrate to align spiritual practices with your holistic health goals.

Reflective Journal Prompt on Spiritual Beliefs and Holistic Health

Consider your spiritual outlook—whether interfaith, nature-based, or entirely personal—and explore how it fosters empathy, community, and inner peace. What experiences have felt most spiritually fulfilling or meaningful to you, and how have they shaped your beliefs or actions?

Exploring Spiritual Beliefs and Holistic Health:

Take a moment to reflect on your core spiritual beliefs. How do these beliefs support or influence your approach to a balanced life incorporating mind, body, and spirit? Write about any insights or actions you can take to align your spiritual practices with your holistic health goals.

- What are my core spiritual beliefs or philosophies?
- How have these beliefs evolved over time?
- Describe an instance where your spiritual beliefs influenced a decision.
- How do your spiritual beliefs align with your current lifestyle, especially concerning holistic health?
- What spiritual practices or rituals do you incorporate into your daily routine, and how do they contribute to your well-being?

Reflective Journaling Questions:

- What experiences in life have felt most spiritually fulfilling to you?
- How do moments of awe or connection with nature influence your beliefs?
- In what ways do you feel connected to something greater than yourself?

Connection to Holistic Health

- In what ways do my spiritual beliefs align with the principles of holistic health?
- How do these beliefs influence my approach to physical, mental, and emotional well-being?

Integration into Daily Life

- What specific activities or rituals help you stay spiritually grounded, and how do they contribute to your mental, emotional, or physical health?

Spiritual clarity often arises from simple acts repeated with meaning—rituals that tether us to purpose and peace. In the next chapter, we'll explore how lifelong learning enriches holistic living. As you nurture your inner growth, you'll gain deeper clarity, compassion, and strength to support every aspect of your well-being. Ready to take the leap? Let's continue this journey together.

CHAPTER 14

CONTINUOUS LEARNING IN HOLISTIC LIVING

In a world that's constantly evolving, our journey toward wellness must evolve too. Continuous learning is the heartbeat of a holistic lifestyle—it invites us to expand, adapt, and deepen our connection to ourselves and the world. Whether through formal study or personal exploration, lifelong learning fuels our capacity to live with intention and vitality. In this chapter, we meet two individuals who embody this spirit.

Case Study:

Isabela, Nutritionist in Buenos Aires, Argentina - A Journey of Continuous Learning

In the vibrant streets of Buenos Aires, Argentina, Isabela's learning style thrived on diversity and immersion. She found inspiration in wellness podcasts, often listening as she tended her balcony garden—a routine that blended reflection with learning. A visual learner at heart, Isabela engaged with colorful infographics and video tutorials that broke down complex nutritional data into digestible insights. Kinesthetically, she loved attending wellness workshops where she could participate in activities like yoga and mindful cooking.

Her interest was piqued by philosophies that integrated well-being across mind, body, and spirit. Isabela was particularly drawn to cross-cultural practices and ancient wisdom, which she seamlessly wove into her work ethos, allowing her to provide clients with enriched solutions that drew upon both modern science and timeless traditions.

Learning from the World

So far, her journey had led her through various holistic disciplines—delving into Ayurveda taught her to appreciate the harmony between food and body. She immersed herself in meditation practices to help clients balance their diets while cultivating peace of mind. These integrated insights began transforming her nutrition practice into holistic wellness coaching, inviting clients to view their health as a multifaceted entity.

A Future Vision: The Ayurvedic Chef Retreat

Looking ahead, Isabela aspired to fulfill her lifelong dream of attending a retreat focused on Ayurvedic principles and culinary arts. She envisioned becoming an Ayurvedic Chef, learning directly from masters in a serene location where the philosophy of balance infused every meal.

This comprehensive learning experience promised to deepen her understanding of food's healing powers and the art of creating nurturing meals tailored to individual constitutions. Isabela's anticipation of this retreat filled her with eager excitement—a new horizon in her learning journey, poised to elevate her skills and broaden her knowledge.

Inspiring Others Through Knowledge and Experience

Isabela's dedication to continuous learning was not solely for personal growth; it was also about sharing her journey and evolving as a professional to empower others. Her openness, adaptability, and curiosity allowed her to be a beacon of inspiration in her community, encouraging others to embrace learning as a lifelong voyage of discovery and transformation.

Her journey underscores that continuous learning in holistic living is an ongoing adventure filled with possibilities—a narrative of growth intertwining personal insight with professional advancement, paving the way for a more balanced and informed existence.

Case Study:

Lucas, Real Estate Broker in Miami, USA - Ongoing Path Towards Holistic Living

In the coastal city of Miami, Florida, Lucas, a former real estate broker, embarked on a daring new venture, driven by his passion for holistic health and personal fitness. Two years ago, he made the bold decision to leave his prosperous real estate career to establish his own holistic health practice—a dream he had cherished since his college days as a football player. However, launching his new venture proved more challenging than anticipated.

Embracing a Diverse Learning Style

Lucas's approach to learning was as dynamic as his career shift. He thrived on kinesthetic learning, which complemented his sports background, excelling in environments where he could actively engage with the material. His days were filled with participation in hands-on workshops, immersive retreats, and online courses covering topics from nutrition science to mental wellness and traditional healing practices. Audiobooks became his companions during early morning runs, providing ongoing education and inspiration.

The embodiment of mind-body harmony resonated deeply with Lucas. He sought knowledge that integrated physical training with wellness philosophies, a balance he yearned to master and share. The blend of sports, personal training, and holistic health became the guiding philosophy for his practice.

Learning Through Experience and Global Perspectives

Over the years, Lucas expanded his knowledge by participating in international marathons—a pursuit that tested his physical endurance while teaching him about perseverance and mental resilience. These experiences provided insights into cultural differences in athletic training and health perspectives, broadening his understanding and empathy as a fitness advisor.

Lucas eagerly connected with mentors worldwide, absorbing a rich tapestry of wisdom that included Eastern meditation techniques, herbal medicine, and modern fitness regimes. His objective was to blend these diverse approaches into a cohesive health practice tailored to the individual needs of his clients.

A Vision for the Future: Retreat in the Caribbean

Lucas's long-term dream is to establish a retreat on a Caribbean island—a haven where people could rejuvenate through his courses on holistic health, fitness training, and wellness. Guests would be immersed in an environment rich with fresh foods, pristine nature, and the company of like-minded individuals. This vision encompasses not only physical transformation but also holistic rejuvenation.

Looking ahead, Lucas is excited about continuing his learning journey. He anticipates collaborating with experts from various disciplines and aims to craft a curriculum for his retreat that reflects the diverse wellness paths he has explored. Lucas is eager to create a sanctuary that empowers others, integrating global wellness strategies with personal growth.

Lucas's story illustrates how a commitment to continuous learning can transform passion into purpose. By embracing diverse educational experiences, he has crafted a holistic philosophy that reflects his evolving understanding. His journey demonstrates that lifelong learning isn't just an ideal; it's a powerful force for sustained growth and fulfillment.

Like Isabela and Lucas, each of us can craft our own path of discovery through learning. The next section offers practical steps to help you begin—or enrich—your own lifelong learning journey.

Review and Implement

Continuous learning nurtures our growth, offering fresh perspectives and insights that enrich our mind, body, and spirit. To embark on this exciting journey, start by setting personal learning goals that resonate deeply with you. Join learning communities where sharing insights and engaging in discussions can amplify your understanding and motivation. Celebrate each milestone reached, recognizing achievements that boost your drive. Stay curious, exploring topics that stretch beyond your current interests and keep the journey vibrant and dynamic.

Synthesize Your Achievements - Ignite Your Next Steps

Quick Checklist

Staying Motivated in a Lifelong Learning Journey

Motivation Tips

- **Set Personal Learning Goals:** Establish clear and meaningful objectives.
- **Engage with a Learning Community:** Join forums or groups for sharing insights.
- **Celebrate Milestones:** Recognize achievements to maintain motivation.
- **Stay Curious:** Explore diverse topics beyond your current interests.

Sample Resource List Tailored to Various Learning Styles

Resources for Visual Learners

Visual resources like online courses, documentaries, and video channels help you grasp holistic health concepts through engaging imagery and clear demonstrations, making it easier to internalize practices and principles.

1. Online Courses

- **Coursera**
  - "The Science of Well-Being" by Yale University[1]
  - "Integrative Health and Medicine" by the University of Minnesota[2]

- **Udemy**
  - "Improve Your Health – Improve Your Life"
  - "Health Coaching Certification Holistic Health Coach Training"

- **Mindvalley**
  - "Free Meditation for Super Performance Masterclass"[3]

2. Documentaries

- "Heal" on PBS: A thoughtful exploration of the mind-body connection and its role in healing.[4]
- "The Sacred Plant" series: A visually rich journey into the cultural roots and healing powers of medicinal plants around the world.[5]

3. YouTube Channels

- Dr. Axe: Health and Wellness[6]
- The Mindful Movement[7]

Resources for Auditory Learners

Podcasts, audiobooks, and webinars support those who learn by listening, offering expert insights and guided reflections that you can absorb on the go or during dedicated listening sessions.

1. Podcasts

- "The Model Health Show"
- "Wellness Mama Podcast"
- "The Rich Roll Podcast" : Discussions on health, wellness, and mindfulness.
- "On Being with Krista Tippett": Exploring the big questions of meaning with varied guests.
- "The Mindful Kind": Tips and insights on mindfulness practices.
- "The Ultimate Health Podcast": Discussions on various health and wellness topics.

2. Audiobooks

- "The Art of Extreme Self-Care" by Cheryl Richardson.
- "The Longevity Diet" by Dr. Valter Longo, available on Audible and other audiobook apps.

3. Webinars

- Integrative Nutrition's Wellness Webinars
- Gaia's Wellness and Self-Growth Webinars

Resources for Kinesthetic Learners

Hands-on workshops, interactive classes, and experiential learning opportunities allow you to embody holistic practices through movement and direct involvement, reinforcing concepts via physical engagement.

1. Workshops

- Local yoga, wellness, and meditation retreats
- Interactive herbalism sessions

2. Hands-On Classes

- Community acupuncture clinics
- Gardening for health workshops

3. Experiential Learning

- **Volunteering at wellness centers:** Participate in classes, events, or client support to apply techniques directly, enhance your practical skills, and build confidence through real-world experiences.

- **Participating in community wellness events:** Engage in local health fairs, group classes, or charity runs to learn by doing, connect with like-minded individuals, and deepen your skills through active participation.

- **Experiences in holistic practices:** Engaging in activities such as crafting herbal remedies, leading guided meditations, or practicing energy healing builds practical skills and enhances personal insight.

Resources for Reading/Writing Learners

Books, articles, and written courses offer detailed information and reflection prompts for those who thrive on reading and writing, enabling you to process ideas at your own pace and deepen your understanding.

1. Books

- "The Mindful Self-Compassion Workbook" by Kristin Neff
- "The Art of Happiness" by the Dalai Lama
- "How to Change Your Mind" by Michael Pollan - Explores the science of psychedelics in wellness
- "The Blue Zones Solution" by Dan Buettner - Lessons from areas with the longest-living populations
- "Healing Spaces: The Science of Place and Well-Being" by Esther M. Sternberg - Illustrated insights on the environment's impact on health

2. Blogs and Articles

- MindBodyGreen
- The Wellness Mama Blog

3. Online Courses

- Berkeley: The Science of Happiness on edX – In-depth written material from Berkeley University on the science of happiness

4. Online Forums

- HealthUnlocked Holistic Health Forum
- Hot Topic - Holistic Health and the Resilient Soldier by the Association of the United States Army (AUSA)

Each step you take expands your potential and brings you closer to the vibrant, balanced life you envision. When learning becomes a way of life, transformation follows naturally.

Shape your unique journey with these tools and strategies, allowing your practice to evolve and nourish every part of you. Reflecting on how continuous learning fuels personal growth and holistic health, we now turn to modern innovations reshaping wellness. In the next chapter, discover how emerging technologies and contemporary methods amplify ancient traditions and open new pathways to well-being. Get ready to explore how timeless wisdom meets tomorrow's breakthroughs, offering tools that elevate our wellness journeys in ways once unimaginable.

CHAPTER 15

INNOVATION AND MODERN SOLUTIONS IN HOLISTIC PRACTICES

Case Study:

Marco, Tech Startup Entrepreneur in Toronto, Canada - Innovating Holistic Health

In the vibrant cityscape of Toronto, Canada, Marco—once the founder of a successful tech startup—faced a health scare that underscored the importance of balance and vitality in life. After selling his company, he redirected his technological expertise towards holistic health, determined to create innovative, tech-driven solutions that promote sustainable well-being.

What was once met with skepticism just a decade ago now commands global attention, and Toronto's culturally diverse and tech-savvy community provides the ideal incubator for his groundbreaking wellness innovations.

Harnessing Technology for Transformation

With his tech background, Marco began exploring how digital platforms and apps could enhance traditional holistic practices. He developed a pilot app that combined personalized wellness plans with real-time data analytics, enabling users to track their mental, physical, and emotional health metrics. This innovative approach allowed individuals to receive tailored health advice, drawing on comprehensive holistic methodologies alongside user-friendly technology.

Marco fueled his learning with a blend of online courses, health tech industry conferences, and consultations with leading holistic practitioners worldwide. His commitment to cross-disciplinary learning kept him at the forefront of new developments, consistently updating his knowledge as technology and wellness intertwined more closely.

Challenges and Milestones in Innovation

One challenge Marco faced was skepticism from conventional health and technology sectors, questioning the viability of integrating such distinct fields. However, his persistence, backed by robust data from successful pilot programs, gradually dispelled doubts. Collaborations with health professionals and technologists globally enriched his projects, solidifying the credibility and reach of his applications.

Towards Global Wellness Integration

Marco aims to establish a global network of wellness communities leveraging technology for enhanced connectivity and improved health outcomes. He envisions creating collaborative spaces where holistic and allopathic practitioners can converge, facilitated by digital platforms that promote learning and health management. Marco is eager to host international symposiums uniting experts in technology, holistic health, and allopathic medicine, aspiring to create an integrated system that delivers the best global wellness knowledge to users worldwide. His work exemplifies how modern innovations are transforming holistic health, using technology to expand traditional practices and inspire next-generation health solutions that are globally informed yet personally tailored.

The Intersection Between Holistic Health and Innovative Technology

These advancements illustrate how innovation can make holistic health more accessible, personalized, and effective—ushering in a new era where wellness is both high-tech and human-centered. Here are some key developments in this realm:

Integrative Health Platforms

Modern health platforms utilize Artificial Intelligence (AI) to integrate data from various sources, such as fitness trackers, genetic profiles, and personal health records, to provide customized wellness plans. These platforms often emphasize preventive health measures, offering personalized insights based on holistic and integrative health principles.

Digital Health Apps

The rise of mobile technology has led to the creation of digital health apps that support mindfulness, meditation, and stress reduction. These apps harness AI to develop personalized meditation routines, track user progress, and provide feedback, facilitating improvements in mental and emotional health.

Telehealth and Virtual Consultations

Telehealth services have expanded access to holistic health practitioners, allowing patients to consult with naturopaths, nutritionists, and wellness coaches online. This technology empowers individuals to receive comprehensive health guidance from the comfort of their homes, breaking down geographical barriers to personalized care.

Functional Health Testing

Platforms like Function Health enable users to go beyond routine medical tests, offering in-depth insights into hormone levels, nutrient deficiencies, and genetic factors.[1]

These tools empower individuals to take proactive steps in their wellness journey with data-driven confidence.

Genomics and Nutrigenomics

Technological advancements have enhanced the study of gene-diet interactions, leading to personalized nutrition plans that improve health based on individual genetic makeup. These fields provide precise strategies for diet and lifestyle modifications aligned with one's genetic predisposition.

Wearable Health Technology

Wearable devices have grown more sophisticated, now capable of monitoring various health metrics such as heart rate variability, sleep patterns, and stress levels. This data allows users and healthcare providers to gain a comprehensive understanding of health that integrates physical, emotional, and even spiritual well-being.

Just as wearable devices monitor physical health in real time, biofeedback technologies offer users direct insight into their mental and physiological states.

Biofeedback and Neurofeedback Devices

These devices provide real-time feedback to help users develop greater awareness and control over physiological functions. By understanding and manipulating biofeedback, users can potentially reduce stress and improve their overall mental health.

Sustainability in Wellness

Innovative building designs and personal spaces utilizing Feng Shui principles promote harmony and energy flow, contributing to a more sustainable lifestyle. This fusion of ancient wisdom with modern eco-friendly practices supports overall well-being.

These designs reflect the growing awareness that our environments profoundly influence our health. By integrating ancient wisdom with modern sustainability principles, we create healing spaces that support physical, mental, and energetic balance.

Through the fusion of technology and holistic health, these innovations not only enhance individual wellness but also pave the way for a holistic health revolution, bringing comprehensive well-being into focus on a global scale.

Visionary: Dr. Mark Hyman

Dr. Hyman is a renowned family physician and a key figure in the functional medicine field.[2] He holds prominent roles, including founder and senior advisor for the Cleveland Clinic Center for Functional Medicine, and director of The UltraWellness Center.[3,4] A vocal advocate for the connection among food, lifestyle, and overall health, Dr. Hyman is also a prolific writer, credited as a 15-time New York Times best-selling author, focusing on topics that bridge the gap between conventional medicine and integrative wellness.

His pioneering work in personalized health is exemplified through Function Health's online lab testing, a transformative healthcare model providing consumers with comprehensive access to a wide array of diagnostics beyond standard insurance-covered tests. This cutting-edge platform enables users to explore hormone levels, nutrient deficiencies, and genetic factors, empowering individuals to take proactive steps in their wellness journey with data-driven confidence.

Extensive Testing and Insights

- **Broad Diagnostic Range**: Unlike traditional healthcare settings that often minimize costs, Function Health's labs provide a vast array of tests that encompass full metabolic panels, hormone levels, and genetic predispositions. This expansive choice ensures users can investigate aspects of their health that aren't typically addressed.

- **Personalized Health Data**: The information gathered from these tests can be shared with primary care physicians or specialists, fostering a collaborative approach to healthcare. This sharing of detailed health insights enhances healthcare providers' ability to craft tailored wellness strategies.

The Role of Technology

- **Cutting-Edge Feedback**: Supported by top-tier global medical professionals, Function Health offers superior analytical feedback. This advanced feedback mechanism leverages global expertise to ensure accuracy and reliability in diagnostics, setting a new standard in health assessments.

- **Future of Medicine**: Pioneers like Dr. Hyman advocate for this integrative approach, emphasizing the role such platforms can play in preventive medicine and long-term health maintenance. By embracing detailed and proactive health monitoring, Function Health aligns with an emerging paradigm focused on holistic well-being rather than reactive treatment.

Through its innovative services, Function Health is reshaping how individuals engage with their health data, promoting an informed and proactive healthcare experience. This initiative represents a significant evolution in personal wellness management, aligning with Dr. Hyman's vision for the future of integrative medicine, where detailed, individualized health insights lead to improved outcomes and enhanced quality of life.

His work reminds us that empowered health decisions start with information—when technology meets functional insight, we gain a roadmap for transformation.

Case Study:

Tania, MD in Boston, USA - Journey from Family Medicine to Holistic Practice

In the historic and bustling city of Boston, Tania, an accomplished MD specializing in family practice, found herself at a critical juncture. Despite her commitment to excellence, the constraints of rushed appointments left both her patients and herself feeling unfulfilled. She recognized the need for a practice model that honored the whole person, not just symptoms. Driven by this insight, Tania envisioned a medical approach centered on holistic health and deeper patient connections.

A New Path Towards Holistic Innovation

With a vision to transform her practice, Tania pursued further studies, focusing on holistic health and the latest innovations in this rapidly evolving sector. Her journey began with a deep dive into integrative medicine, where she explored how modern technology could complement traditional holistic practices.

Leveraging Technology and Realizing Dreams

Tania discovered a range of digital tools and wellness apps, such as personalized meditation platforms and holistic health trackers, designed to integrate seamlessly into daily life. These innovations allowed her to experiment with new ways to manage stress, both for herself and as recommendations for her patients. She was particularly intrigued by advances in AI-driven health analytics, which offered tailored wellness plans based on individual health metrics and lifestyle data.

A standout innovation that captured Tania's attention was a cutting-edge research study on virtual reality (VR) as a tool for stress reduction and mental health support. Recognized for its potential to create immersive meditative experiences that engage all senses, VR promised an exciting avenue to explore holistic therapy in a rapidly changing digital landscape.

For instance, a patient struggling with anxiety might engage in a 10-minute VR experience simulating a peaceful forest walk—promoting calm, focus, and nervous system regulation before a consultation.

Tackling Chronic Illnesses with Holistic Insight

Another significant aspect of Tania's focus was dissecting the root causes of chronic illnesses, such as hypertension, diabetes, autoimmune issues, and hormonal and thyroid imbalances that have proliferated in recent years. She invested time in researching lifestyle interventions that address these conditions before they manifest fully. Innovations in genomics and nutrigenomics particularly captivated her, highlighting how dietary adjustments tailored to genetic information could effectively avert such illnesses.

Challenges, Discoveries, and Wins

The road was not without its challenges. Tania faced the uphill battle of integrating these new technologies into a traditionally structured healthcare system. Overcoming skepticism was part of her journey; however, her unwavering commitment gradually bore fruit as she showcased tangible results. By piloting tech-assisted wellness programs within her practice, Tania demonstrated improved patient outcomes, notably in managing anxiety and fostering healthier lifestyles.

Her participation in global forums on holistic health innovation allowed her to connect with pioneers across various disciplines, broadening her perspective and enhancing her practice with multicultural insights and solutions. These collaborations illuminated the shared aspirations within the health industry to bridge innovation with tradition for comprehensive care.

A Vision for the Future

Tania's ultimate dream is to establish a holistic health practice where she can dedicate meaningful time to understanding each patient's journey, practicing medicine with the depth and empathy she envisions. This practice would leverage technology not as a replacement but as an ally, augmenting comprehensive health management with a personal touch—an embodiment of holistic health in the modern age.

Visionary: Dr. Michelle Sands

Dr. Sands is a well-regarded authority in hormone and thyroid health, dedicated to enhancing patient care through a holistic approach. Holding a doctorate in naturopathic medicine, Dr. Sands possesses a robust understanding of both traditional and alternative health disciplines. This comprehensive education enables her to create individualized strategies tailored to her patients' needs, focusing particularly on hormone balance and the intricate interactions within the thyroid system. As a strong advocate for integrating lifestyle changes, nutritional adjustments, and mind-body practices into medical treatments, Dr. Sands empowers patients to take an active role in their health journey. Through her numerous publications and public speaking engagements, Dr. Sands diligently demystifies hormone health, making it accessible and understandable to wider audiences. Her work fosters a deeper public consciousness about hormone-related issues, encouraging informed decisions and healthier lifestyles.[5]

Expert in Toxin-free Hormone and Thyroid Health

- **Personalized Treatments:** Dr. Sands emphasizes individualized health solutions, recognizing that hormonal and thyroid conditions vary widely among individuals. By assessing each person's unique hormonal profile, she tailors treatments to address specific needs, thereby enhancing overall health outcomes. Her online platform, Glow Natural Wellness, seamlessly facilitates clients' access to continuous education and treatment protocols, backed by a top-tier support team available 24/7.[6]

- **Education and Advocacy:** A key component of Dr. Sands's work is educating her patients and the broader public about the critical role hormones play in maintaining health and vitality. Her efforts extend to workshops, speaking engagements, and written resources, all aimed at demystifying hormonal health and empowering individuals to take charge of their wellness.

Approach and Innovations

- **Functional Medicine Perspective:** Dr. Sands adopts a functional medicine approach, focusing on the root causes of hormonal imbalances rather than merely treating symptoms. This methodology explores the interplay between hormones, diet, lifestyle, and environmental factors to foster a comprehensive healing process.

- **Integrative Health Strategies:** Combining traditional medical knowledge with integrative therapies, Dr. Sands's work encompasses various treatments, including dietary modifications, nutritional supplements, and lifestyle interventions, all designed to support hormonal balance and enhance thyroid function.

Contributions and Impact

Dr. Sands' commitment to advancing hormone and thyroid health is reflected in her proactive stance on patient education and her advocacy for personalized medicine. Her holistic approach not only addresses current health challenges but also promotes long-term wellness, positioning her as an influential voice in the health community dedicated to transforming lives through informed health choices.

By integrating scientific precision with personalized care, Dr. Sands models the future of holistic medicine—accessible, tailored, and deeply human.

Genomics and Nutrigenomics

Genomics and nutrigenomics are rapidly evolving fields that offer personalized insights into how our genes interact with nutrition, shaping how we prevent and manage disease. Both fields leverage advanced technologies like next-generation sequencing and bioinformatics to analyze DNA and identify genetic markers relevant to health and nutrition. These technologies facilitate understanding complex biological processes and enhance the accuracy of nutritional interventions.

Genomics

Genomics is the comprehensive study of an individual's entire genetic makeup—mapping, sequencing, and analyzing the genome to reveal how genes influence traits and disease risk. By uncovering these genetic insights, genomics drives personalized medicine, enabling tailored healthcare strategies, targeted therapies, and informed risk assessments for hereditary conditions. It also powers pharmacogenomics, optimizing drug selection and dosing by examining how genes affect metabolism and treatment response.

Nutrigenomics

Nutrigenomics explores how our diet influences gene activity and how genetic variations shape nutritional needs and disease risk. By leveraging next-generation sequencing and bioinformatics to analyze these gene–nutrient interactions, it enables personalized nutrition plans that optimize metabolic health, support weight management, and prevent chronic conditions. This tailored approach aligns dietary recommendations with each individual's genetic profile, offering precise strategies for lasting wellness.

Integration and Future Outlook

Personalized Nutrition and Medicine:

The integration of genomics and nutrigenomics into healthcare marks a new era of precision nutrition and medicine. This evolution aims to create interventions and lifestyle modifications tailored to an individual's genetic makeup, thereby optimizing health outcomes.

Potential and Challenges:

As research progresses, addressing concerns around privacy, ethics, and complexity will be crucial to making personalized nutrition accessible, safe, and empowering for all.

Overall, genomics and nutrigenomics signify significant advancements in understanding how our genetic blueprint interacts with diet and health. As research continues to evolve, these fields have the potential to transform our approach to nutrition and healthcare on a personal level.

Review and Implement

Ethical Implications of Technology in Holistic Health

Before delving into specifics, let's consider the ethical implications of combining technology with holistic health. Reflecting on issues such as data privacy, equity, and cultural respect ensures that our well-being practices uplift everyone involved.

- **Privacy Concerns:** Managing sensitive health data carefully while ensuring user confidentiality.
- **Dependence on Technology:** Balancing technology use with traditional holistic practices to avoid over-reliance.
- **Equity of Access:** Ensuring equal access to digital health tools for all demographics.

By keeping these considerations at the forefront, we can ensure our innovations serve everyone with compassion and fairness.

Embody Your Vision - Ignite Your Purpose

Quick Checklist

Examples of Apps and Tools Aligning with Holistic Principles

Headspace: Guided meditations and mindfulness exercises for stress relief, focus, and better sleep, featuring themed courses and progress tracking.[7]

Calm: Provides guided meditations, sleep stories, and breathing exercises with daily mindfulness reminders to reduce stress and enhance sleep.[8]

Insight Timer: Offers a vast library of diverse meditations, a customizable timer, and community groups led by expert instructors.[9]

MyFitnessPal: Allows easy calorie and nutrient tracking, barcode scanning, and device syncing to support personalized nutrition and fitness goals.[10]

As we embrace new tools and insights, we recognize that innovation complements ancient wisdom—it enhances our wellness journey, allowing us to evolve. Whether through mindful app use or ethical tech practices, the key is to let innovation support your wellness, not replace it.

Having explored the role of innovation in enhancing holistic health practices, we now shift our focus to a crucial aspect of maintaining these advancements: committing to your holistic journey. In the next chapter, we delve into actionable strategies that foster a steadfast commitment to wellness. Discover how integrating these practices with personal goals and consistency can lead to lasting improvements in your health and overall life satisfaction.

CHAPTER 16

COMMITTING TO YOUR HOLISTIC JOURNEY

Case Study:

Michael, Hospitality Executive in Dubai, UAE - Innovator for Global Cultural Wellness Experiences

In the opulent corridors of Dubai's thriving hospitality industry, Michael, a seasoned executive from San Diego, discovered a deeper vision for revolutionizing global wellness tourism. During his time in the region, he witnessed its transformation into a booming hub for health and wellness, inspired by innovative blends of hospitality and holistic service offerings. His extensive career, spanning luxury resort management to strategic roles in international hotel chains, instilled in him the principles of exceptional guest service and luxurious accommodation.

At the Forefront of Industry Evolution

Michael's distinguished career was marked by critical insights, particularly as he observed the rise of wellness tourism in Dubai. His curiosity was piqued by the growing interest in wellness retreats in the Red Sea region, especially after engaging with an innovative collective exploring the fusion of luxury and holistic experiences. Motivated by these fresh ideas, Michael devised a novel blueprint for his future endeavors—a comprehensive wellness retreat project that intertwined archaeology, astrology, oceanic explorations, and culinary arts into a vibrant cultural narrative. His goal was to attract those disenchanted with the Western capitalist model of luxury, seeking authentic adventures over superficial amenities.

Transitioning to a Holistic Vision

Upon returning to North America, settling in Miami provided a strategic base for Michael's transition from corporate hospitality to holistic retreat experiences. This shift required meticulous planning and collaboration with pioneering figures in wellness tourism, revealing the industry's vast potential as a transformative force. Moreover, Michael navigated complex bureaucratic processes in the Middle East, recognizing that while challenging, these intricacies were easing as global interconnectedness increased.

Challenges and Discoveries Along the Way

Michael faced numerous challenges, particularly in shifting from a traditional corporate mindset to embracing holistic values. Attending global wellness and hospitality conferences expanded his understanding of the synergy between lifestyle industries and enriched his strategic vision. This comprehensive research informed his framework for sustainable retreat models that accommodate diverse guest needs, promoting overall well-being.

Wins and Empowering Communities

In Miami, Michael initiated small wellness seminars, envisioning a future retreat where guests would participate in locally enriched activities and innovative health practices. Collaborating with architects and wellness experts, he developed plans for a sanctuary emphasizing simplicity over extravagance, offering an alternative to mainstream wellness experiences. His initial sketches depicted Bedouin tents and fireside cooking circles—a nod to traditional Bedouin customs, inviting all travelers to share in food and community.

Michael's expansive vision transcended conventional luxury, embracing a community-oriented strategy that immerses guests in local ecology and culture while advocating for sustainable tourism. The integration of art, music, and gastronomy within his offerings crystallized an integrative approach to wellness.

A Vision Realized: Future Dreams

Looking ahead, Michael plans to expand his retreat offerings by partnering with local communities and exploring new natural settings, ensuring that more people can access these transformative practices. He envisions a future where shared healing journeys are available to all, fostering widespread renewal and connection.

Michael aspires to realize this vision in the enchanting Red Sea region, rich in history and natural beauty. He envisions a retreat that weaves cultural heritage into personalized wellness experiences—blending natural splendor, ancestral wisdom, and community connection. By forging partnerships with airlines and regional businesses, he is determined to make authentic, transformative journeys accessible to everyone. This unwavering dedication has not only redirected his career but also deepened his personal insights, demonstrating that steadfast commitment can create genuinely transformative hospitality.

Michael's journey illustrates how experienced professionals can reinvent themselves by aligning their expertise with a commitment to holistic living, raising the bar for wellness tourism and inspiring others to embark on their own meaningful transformations.

Case Study*:

[Real scenario – resonated with many during the COVID epidemic, on a path toward self-discovery at a time when people around the world were searching for honesty, questioning whom to trust, and feeling completely vulnerable and lost. Oliver, you struck a global nerve—thank you for your courage and for daring to share your own pain for the benefit of so many others needing your "reality" perspective to survive.]

Oliver Bowers in Kent, England: Creator of Walk the Mind

Life-Altering Experience

In the quiet town of Folkestone, Kent, Oliver Bowers was once an ordinary teenager navigating the challenges of adolescence—until, at age 16, he experienced a traumatic event that shifted his world. This incident left invisible scars and planted the seeds of post-traumatic stress, manifesting as emotional detachment and persistent anxiety. For years, Oliver carried these burdens in silence, unsure of their origin, until in adulthood, he sought help and began to unravel the weight he had long borne alone.

The Healing Path of CBT and Nature

Oliver's turning point came through cognitive behavioral therapy (CBT), a structured form of psychotherapy that helped him confront his trauma and reframe his thought patterns. As part of his therapeutic journey, he began taking long walks with his puppy, Ted. These walks transformed into moments of mindfulness and emotional release.

Walking along the chalky coastal trails of Folkestone, through the green hills and along the tranquil seafront of the English Channel, provided him space to breathe, reflect, and reconnect with the present. The rhythm of walking—one step at a time—mirrored the steady pace of recovery. With every mile, Oliver noticed his anxiety ease and his mood lift. The natural environment became both a sanctuary and a silent therapist.

Birth of Walk the Mind

Recognizing the transformative power of these mindful walks, Oliver felt a growing desire to share this healing practice with others. In 2019, from the comfort of his Folkestone home, he launched Walk the Mind, a social media-based community designed to support individuals struggling with mental health.[1]

What began as a small, local Facebook group quickly evolved into a global platform where people could post photos of their walks, exchange stories, and offer each other encouragement. The ethos was simple yet heartfelt: walking with intention could restore clarity, relieve emotional pain, and build connections.

Walk The Mind wasn't about hiking marathons or fitness goals—it aimed to create a safe, inclusive space where mental health conversations could flourish alongside lived experiences.

Community and Global Impact

Oliver's vision resonated deeply. Within a year, Walk the Mind grew to over 30,000 members from more than 120 countries. Thousands of individuals—many of whom had never spoken openly about their mental health before—found solace in sharing their daily walks and reading others' journeys.

In Folkestone and the surrounding Dover area alone, around 7,000 members participated. Oliver regularly organized community walks and fundraising events, including walking one million steps in a month and leading group walks that raised awareness and funds for Young Minds, a leading UK mental health charity.2 He raised over £11,000 and, in 2020, was recognized as a finalist for the Meridian Pride of Britain Fundraiser of the Year.3

A Future Built on Purpose

Even as Walk the Mind gained national recognition, Oliver remained grounded, continuing his regular job in Dover while volunteering as club secretary for the local Cinque Ports Football Club.[4] His passion for mental health advocacy only deepened.

He later enrolled at Canterbury Christ Church University, studying to become a counselor. His goal was to expand Walk the Mind from a grassroots movement into a fully registered charity, offering workshops in schools, corporate wellness programs, and research-based education on how walking and nature support emotional resilience.[5]

Legacy of One Step

Oliver Bowers' story reminds us that healing doesn't always come in grand gestures—it can begin with something as simple as putting one foot in front of the other. Through Walk The Mind, he has empowered thousands to reclaim mental wellness through mindful movement and collective support.

From the seafront trails of Kent to digital spaces around the world, Oliver has built a legacy grounded in empathy, courage, and community—a legacy that continues to grow, one step at a time.

His journey reminds us that sometimes the simplest actions lead us to our purpose—an idea beautifully echoed in the Japanese philosophy of Ikigai.

Ikigai - A Daily Reminder of Your Why

Ikigai is a Japanese concept that encapsulates living a life driven by purpose and fulfillment. Often translated as "reason for being," Ikigai combines the Japanese words *iki* (life) and *gai* (worth). This philosophy is seen as central to achieving balance and harmony in all aspects of life, influencing dimensions of existence from career choices to personal relationships.[6]

For instance, someone who loves teaching and has a gift for communication might find their Ikigai by offering free wellness workshops in their community—fulfilling both their passion and a public need.

The Four Pillars of Ikigai

Ikigai is framed by four core elements that converge to bring meaning and satisfaction:

1. **What You Love (Passion):** Reflecting on activities and interests you are genuinely passionate about, this pillar encourages engagement in work and hobbies that bring joy and fulfillment.

2. **What You Are Good At (Vocation):** This pillar emphasizes leveraging your skills and talents, encouraging the pursuit of endeavors where strengths align with tasks, driving personal growth and expertise.

3. **What You Can Be Paid For (Profession):** This dimension assesses economic realities, suggesting that sustainable income aligns with purpose-driven activities, creating a harmonious work-life balance.

4. **What the World Needs (Mission):** It aligns personal purpose with broader societal needs, suggesting contributions that positively impact the world and resonate with community values.

The intersection of these four pillars represents one's Ikigai, a sweet spot that offers a fulfilling and balanced life.

Living by Ikigai

In practice, identifying and nurturing one's Ikigai involves introspection and alignment of personal values with daily activities. It is an iterative journey, inviting individuals to pursue what they passionately love while contributing value to society and maintaining financial viability.

Impact on Well-Being

- **Enhancing Happiness and Health:** Studies show that individuals who embrace Ikigai feel more satisfied and approach life with purpose, which is linked to increased longevity and overall well-being.
- **Building Resilience:** An Ikigai-centered lifestyle provides resilience to face challenges, anchoring individuals to a meaningful cause that motivates perseverance during difficult times.
- **Promoting Contentment:** By integrating Ikigai into daily life, people find satisfaction not just in

reaching end goals but also through the process itself, cultivating gratitude and presence in everyday encounters.

A Global Perspective

While Ikigai is rooted in Japanese culture, its universal principles have gained global appreciation. It serves as a powerful tool for anyone seeking greater harmony and clarity about their life's path, offering actionable insights for achieving personal fulfillment and a balanced lifestyle.

For example, in the olive groves of southern Italy, farmers embody Ikigai by blending their passion for cultivation and expertise in traditional methods to produce olive oil that sustains both their families and the local community—demonstrating how Ikigai's pillars translate into diverse cultural practices.

Review and Implement

Embarking on a long-term holistic journey takes commitment and requires the ability to navigate its accompanying challenges, including:

Lifestyle Adjustments: Transitioning to a holistic lifestyle often requires significant changes in daily habits, such as diet, exercise, and stress management. Committing to these changes can be challenging, especially when balancing them with existing responsibilities and routines.

Overcoming Skepticism: Individuals may face skepticism from others about their holistic choices, particularly if these diverge from mainstream approaches. Building confidence in one's path and staying committed despite external doubts can be daunting.

Access and Resources: When access feels limited, consider exploring free or low-cost alternatives—stream guided sessions online, borrow library books on holistic practices, join neighborhood wellness meetups in local parks, or start a small group with friends at home. These simple steps can provide meaningful support and keep you connected to your holistic journey.

Consistency and Dedication: Holistic health is an ongoing commitment that requires dedication and consistency. Maintaining motivation during moments of doubt or difficulty is crucial for sustaining progress on the journey.

Emotional and Spiritual Challenges: A holistic journey often prompts deep emotional and spiritual exploration, which can bring unresolved issues and emotions to the surface. Navigating these challenges requires mindfulness, resilience, and sometimes the support of mental health professionals or spiritual guides.

Commitment to the Journey - Purpose and Meaning

Viktor Frankl, an Austrian neurologist and psychologist, emphasized that true fulfillment lies not in the absence of difficulty but in striving towards meaningful goals. His teachings remind us that embracing challenges and uncovering purpose is at the heart of a truly satisfying life.[7]

To stay committed to long-term goals, combining introspective tools like *Ikigai* with structured methods such as SMART goals (Specific, Measurable, Achievable, Relevant, Time-Bound) can be beneficial. Regular reflection, community support, and digital planning tools help maintain direction, motivation, and consistency.

Celebrate Milestones - Embrace Continued Growth

Quick Checklist

Motivational Checklist to Review When You Feel Off Track

Reconnect with Your Why:

- Reflect on your original motivation for embracing holistic living.

Set Intentions

- Define what holistic health means to you and establish clear intentions for your journey.

Start Small

- **Begin with Manageable Practices:** Commit to small, regular actions that are sustainable.

- **Celebrate Progress:** Acknowledge achievements, however minor—they signify momentum.
- **Reconnect with Your Why:** Reflect on what inspired your journey.
- **Engage with Supportive Communities:** Surround yourself with like-minded individuals who uplift your growth.
- **Reassess as You Grow:** Regularly check in on your goals, adapting your path with grace and flexibility.

Embrace Consistency

- Commitment to regular practice and reflection ensures sustained growth and benefits.

Stay Open-Minded

- Remain receptive to learning and adapting as you explore various aspects of holistic health.

Practice Self-Compassion:

- Treat yourself with kindness and understanding during setbacks.

Reassess and Adjust:

- Periodically evaluate your goals and strategies, making adjustments as needed.

Engage with Supportive Communities:

- Connect with like-minded individuals for encouragement and accountability.

As you reflect on these guiding practices, remember that true commitment arises not from perfection but from showing up with intention each day.

As we conclude this book, I invite you to embark on a transformative journey of personal growth and holistic exploration. This marks not just the end of a book but the beginning of a lifelong commitment to nurturing your body, mind, and spirit. Armed with insights, global journeys, sample case studies, and actionable items outlined in these pages, you are now equipped to unlock your fullest potential. You've done more than read—you've reflected, practiced, and planted seeds for transformation. Know that wherever you are in your journey, the steps you've taken matter and will continue to unfold in powerful ways. Consider:

- **Achievements:** Reflect on what you have accomplished by implementing the action items.
- **Learnings:** Revisit what you've learned from our shared travels through fascinating places and the historical context of the philosophies discussed.

- **Integrating Ideals:** Contemplate your insights from synthesizing modern innovations with timeless wisdom and consider the future direction this points you toward.

Every day presents a fresh opportunity for learning, healing, and embracing the holistic path to fulfillment. Remember, this is just the start of a rewarding journey toward richer well-being and profound self-discovery.

Your journey matters deeply to me. Let's continue growing together—your voice, story, and dreams belong in this shared space of healing and possibility.

BIBLIOGRAPHY

Chapter 1

1. Elendu, C. (2024). The evolution of ancient healing practices: From shamanism to Hippocratic medicine: A review. *Medicine, 103*(28), e39005. https://doi.org/10.1097/md.0000000000039005

2. Mythology, E. (2024, September 7). The temple of Imhotep at Saqqara: A look at the divine healer's sanctuary. *Egypt Mythology*. https://egyptmythology.com/the-temple-of-imhotep-at-saqqara-a-look-at-the-divine-healers-sanctuary/

3. Ayurveda: A brief introduction and guide. (2024, January 8). *Ayurveda*. https://ayurveda.com/ayurveda-a-brief-introduction-and-guide/

4. Sharma, H. (2016). Ayurveda: Science of life, genetics, and epigenetics. *AYU: An International Quarterly Journal of Research in Ayurveda, 37*(2), 87. https://doi.org/10.4103/ayu.ayu_220_16

5. Murray, J. (2019, June 25). Daoist mysticism. *Oxford Research Encyclopedia of Religion*. https://ox-

fordre.com/religion/view/10.1093/acre-
fore/9780199340378.001.0001/acrefore-
9780199340378-e-136

Chapter 2

1. SushiLaya. (2024, February 25). A complete tour
   guide to Lumbini: The birthplace of Gautama
   Buddha. *Inside Himalayas*. https://www.in-
   sidehimalayas.com/a-complete-tour-guide-to-lum-
   bini-the-birthplace-of-gautama-buddha/

2. Sedlmeier, P., Beckel, A., Conrad, S., Husmann, J.,
   Kullrich, L., Lange, R., Müller, A., Neumann, A.,
   Schaaf, T., Schaub, A., Tränkner, A., & Witzel, B.
   (2023). Mindfulness meditation according to the
   Satipatthana Sutta: A single-case study with participants as collaborators. *Mindfulness, 14*(7), 1636–
   1649. https://doi.org/10.1007/s12671-023-
   02160-1

3. Hearst agrees to acquire Rodale Inc.'s global content business. (n.d.). *Hearst*.
   https://www.hearst.com/-/hearst-agrees-to-ac-
   quire-rodale-inc-s-global-content-business

4. Janssen, M., Heerkens, Y., Kuijer, W., van der Hei-
   jden, B., & Engels, J. (2018). Effects of mindfulness-based stress reduction on employees' mental
   health: A systematic review. *PLoS ONE, 13*(1),

e0191332. https://doi.org/10.1371/jour-nal.pone.0191332

5. Zhang, D., Lee, E. K. P., Mak, E. C. W., Ho, C. Y., & Wong, S. Y. S. (2021). Mindfulness-based interventions: An overall review. *British Medical Bulletin, 138*(1), 41–57. https://doi.org/10.1093/bmb/ldab005

6. Lu, C., Dijk, S. W., Pandit, A., Kranenburg, L., Luik, A. I., & Hunink, M. G. M. (2023). The effect of mindfulness-based interventions on reducing stress in future health professionals: A systematic review and meta-analysis of randomized controlled trials. *Applied Psychology: Health and Well-Being, 16*(2), 765–792. https://doi.org/10.1111/aphw.12472

7. Lueke, A., & Gibson, B. (2015). Mindfulness meditation reduces implicit age and race bias: The role of reduced automaticity of responding. *Social Psychological and Personality Science, 6*(3), 284–291. https://doi.org/10.1177/1948550614559651

8. Liu, S., Xin, H., Shen, L., He, J., & Liu, J. (2020). The influence of individual and team mindfulness on work engagement. *Frontiers in Psychology, 10*. https://doi.org/10.3389/fpsyg.2019.02928

9. He, J., Li, X., Wang, H., & Xu, Z. (2023). A study on the relationship between mindfulness and work

performance of web editors: Based on the chain mediating effect of workplace spirituality and digital competencies. *Frontiers in Psychology, 13.* https://doi.org/10.3389/fpsyg.2022.1068735

10. Prakash, R. S., Fountain-Zaragoza, S., Kramer, A. F., Samimy, S., & Wegman, J. (2020). Mindfulness and attention: Current state of affairs and future considerations. *Journal of Cognitive Enhancement, 4*(3), 340–367. https://doi.org/10.1007/s41465-019-00144-5

11. Capurso, V., Fabbro, F., & Crescentini, C. (2014). Mindful creativity: The influence of mindfulness meditation on creative thinking. *Frontiers in Psychology, 4.* https://doi.org/10.3389/fpsyg.2013.01020

Chapter 3

1. Peace Corps. (n.d.). Agriculture and environment extension agent. *Peace Corps.* https://www.peace-corps.gov/ways-to-serve/service-assignments/browse-opportunities/peace-corps-volunteer/agriculture-and-environment-extension-agent-9351br/

2. itrvl client portal. (n.d.). https://itrvl.com/client/example/645df26ad0fb69005e66bee7/609478128ea27

400618740d4/609478138ea27400618740d5

3. Natural Habitat Adventures. (n.d.). Conservation: Electric safari vehicle. https://www.nathab.com/conservation/electric-safari-vehicle/

4. Wilderness. (n.d.). DumaTau: Where elephant herds cross ancient African corridors. https://www.wildernessdestinations.com/africa/botswana/linyanti-region/dumatau-camp/

5. Wilderness. (n.d.). DumaTau – Enjoy. https://wetu.com/iBrochure/en/Information/9986/DumaTau_Camp/Activities

6. Sacred Land. (n.d.). Tsodilo Hills – Botswana. https://sacredland.org/tsodilo-hills-botswana/

7. Crookedadmin. (2024, April 2). The story of the San Bushmen. *Crooked Compass*. https://www.crooked-compass.com/travel-blog/story-of-the-san-bushmen/

8. University of Oslo. (n.d.). World's oldest ritual discovered: Worshipped the python 70,000 years ago. https://www.apollon.uio.no/english/articles/2006/python-english.html

9. Kaza. (2023, December 15). Tsodilo Hills: A sacred legacy of the San people and their spiritual

heart. *Uncover Kavango Zambezi.*
https://www.uncoverkaza.com/tsodilo-hills-a-sa-cred-legacy-of-the-san-people-and-their-spiritual-heart/

10. Wilderness. (n.d.). Mokoro excursions.
https://www.wildernessdestinations.com/experi-ences/safari/mokoro

11. Wilderness. (n.d.). Star beds. https://www.wilder-nessdestinations.com/experiences/safari/star-beds

12. Paumelle, J., & Garat, H. (2020). *Paris climate action plan: Towards a carbon neutral city, 100% renewable energies, resilient, fair and inclusive.*
https://cdn.paris.fr/paris/2020/11/23/a10afc931be2124e21e39a1624132724.pdf

13. SushiLaya. (2024, February 25). A complete tour guide to Lumbini: The birthplace of Gautama Buddha. *Inside Himalayas.* https://www.in-sidehimalayas.com/a-complete-tour-guide-to-lum-bini-the-birthplace-of-gautama-buddha/

14. Yarbrough, M. (2024, November 13). Unlock the power of Egyptian meditation techniques today!
Medium. https://me-dium.com/@meyarbrough_55952/unlock-the-power-of-egyptian-meditation-techniques-today-8116503620f6

15. Parrot, S. (2024, April 5). Kemetic meditation: Ancient Egyptian techniques for modern minds. *The Spiritual Parrot*. https://thespiritualparrot.com/kemetic-meditation-ancient-egyptian-techniques-for-modern-minds/#google_vignette

16. Transcendental Meditation Technique – Official website. (n.d.). https://www.tm.org/homepage-1?va-red=MTU2MDQ6MjE3MTA

17. Thomas, L. (2021, February 7). Watch David Lynch and Paul McCartney discuss the world of 'Transcendental Meditation'. *Far Out Magazine*. https://faroutmagazine.co.uk/david-lynch-paul-mccartney-meditation-talk/

18. Conti, G., Doyle, O., Fearon, P., & Oppedisano, V. (2022). A demonstration study of the quiet time transcendental meditation program. *Frontiers in Psychology, 12.* https://doi.org/10.3389/fpsyg.2021.765158

19. Dass, R. (2010). *Be here now*. Harmony.

Chapter 4

1. Office of the Commissioner. (2021, July 1). Grapefruit juice and some drugs don't mix. *U.S. Food and Drug Administration.*

https://www.fda.gov/consumers/consumer-up-dates/grapefruit-juice-and-some-drugs-dont-mix

2. Thiele, J. (2024, May 20). A guide for herb-drug interactions. *Herbal Reality*. https://www.herb-alreality.com/herbalism/safety/a-guide-for-herb-drug-interactions/

Chapter 5

1. Basque Administration Web Portal. (n.d.). City wall of Hondarribia. *Tourism Euskadi*. https://tourism.euskadi.eus/en/cultural-heri-tage/city-wall-of-hondarribia/webtur00-con-tent/en/

2. Hondarribia's defensive wall – Gipuzkoa. (n.d.). http://www.gipuzkoamuseobirtu-ala.net/teselas8527.html

3. Goitur. (2025a, January 23). Goierri's symbol: Latxa sheep. *Goierri Turismo*. Retrieved April 7, 2025, from https://goierriturismo.com/en/na-ture-en/goierris-symbol-latxa-sheep/

4. Goitur. (2025b, January 31). Idiazabal: Awarded cheese. *Goierri Turismo*. Retrieved April 7, 2025, from https://goierriturismo.com/en/gastron-omy/idiazabal-awarded-cheese/

5. Guide du Pays Basque. (n.d.). Hondarribia, medieval, maritime and gastronomic town. https://www.guide-du-paysbasque.com/en/experiences/culture-and-heritage/article-hondarribia-medieval-maritime-and-gastronomic-town-353.html

6. Anne-Marie. (2019, August 27). 5 facts about Euskara, the Basque language. *Hella Basque*. https://www.hellabasque.org/euskara-facts/

7. Kuta, S. (2024, February 21). Words etched into an ancient bronze hand hint at the mysterious origins of the Basque language. *Smithsonian Magazine*. https://www.smithsonianmag.com/smart-news/words-etched-into-an-ancient-bronze-hand-hint-at-the-mysterious-origins-of-the-basque-language-180981153/

8. Otazu, A., Otazu, A., & Otazu, A. (2022, November 28). The Hand of Irulegi delivers more questions than answers on Basque origins. *EL PAÍS English*. https://english.elpais.com/culture/2022-11-28/the-hand-of-irulegi-delivers-more-questions-than-answers-on-basque-origins.html

9. Ochoa, B., García-Diez, M., & Vigiola-Toña, I. (2020). Filling the void: A new Palaeolithic cave art site at Danbolinzulo in the Basque Country. *Antiquity, 94*(373), 27–43.

https://doi.org/10.15184/aqy.2019.236

10. The Hungry Tourist Ltd. (2024, March 5). The very best of Basque Country food. *The Hungry Tourist*. https://thehungrytourist.com/the-very-best-of-basque-country-food/

11. National Heart, Lung, and Blood Institute. (2022, March 24). Your sleep/wake cycle. *National Institutes of Health*. https://www.nhlbi.nih.gov/health/sleep/sleep-wake-cycle

12. Vertebral Subluxation Research. (2020, August 25). Resolution of hypothyroidism & dysautonomia following chiropractic care to reduce vertebral subluxation: A case study & review of literature. https://vertebralsubluxationre-search.com/2020/08/25/resolution-of-hypothy-roidism-dysautonomia-following-chiropractic-care-to-reduce-vertebral-subluxation-a-case-study-review-of-literature/

13. Kurth, S. (2022, September 13). 3 reasons to choose chiropractic care for thyroid conditions. *Apex Chiropractic*. https://apexchiroco.com/up-dates/3-reasons-to-choose-chiropractic-care-for-thyroid-conditions/

14. Vertebral Subluxation Research. (2017, October 27). Resolution of hypothyroidism & irritable

bowel syndrome in a 34-year-old female following chiropractic care to reduce vertebral subluxation: A case study & review of the literature. https://vertebralsubluxationre-search.com/2017/10/27/resolution-of-hypothy-roidism-irritable-bowel-syndrome-in-a-34-year-old-female-following-chiropractic-care-to-reduce-vertebral-subluxation-a-case-study-review-of-the-literature/

Chapter 6

1. GW Today. (n.d.). How to manage in a world of digital overload. https://gwtoday.gwu.edu/how-manage-world-digital-overload

2. Park, J. H., Moon, J. H., Kim, H. J., Kong, M. H., & Oh, Y. H. (2020). Sedentary lifestyle: Overview of updated evidence of potential health risks. *Korean Journal of Family Medicine, 41*(6), 365–373. https://doi.org/10.4082/kjfm.20.0165

3. Chang, C., Lin, B. B., Feng, X., Andersson, E., Gardner, J., & Astell-Burt, T. (2024). A lower connection to nature is related to lower mental health benefits from nature contact. *Scientific Reports, 14*(1). https://doi.org/10.1038/s41598-024-56968-5

4. Roberts, B. L., & Karatsoreos, I. N. (2021). Brain–body responses to chronic stress: A brief review.

Faculty Reviews, 10.
https://doi.org/10.12703/r/10-83

Chapter 7

1. Conservation International. (n.d.). Sustainable living tips. https://www.conservation.org/act/sustainable-living-tips

2. Adler, L. (2025, January 13). *Home.* https://www.laraadler.com/

3. Institute of Nutritional Endocrinology. (2025, April 21). Restore metabolic health, energy & rebalance your hormones. *Dr. Ritamarie Loscalzo.* https://drritamarie.com/

4. HeartMath Institute. (n.d.). HeartMath Institute. https://www.heartmath.org/

5. Cleveland Clinic. (2025a, January 6). Detox or cleanse: What to know before you start. https://health.clevelandclinic.org/detox-cleanse

6. Visioli, F., Mucignat-Caretta, C., Anile, F., & Panaite, S. (2022). Traditional and medical applications of fasting. *Nutrients, 14*(3), 433. https://doi.org/10.3390/nu1403043

7. Massachusetts Institute of Technology. (2024, August 21). Study reveals the benefits and downside

of fasting. *MIT News.*
https://news.mit.edu/2024/study-reveals-fasting-benefits-and-downside-0821

8. Stem Cell Research Center. (2025, January 7). Top 6 ways to boost your stem cells naturally. *The Regeneration Center.* https://stemcellthai-land.org/6-ways-boost-stem-cells-naturally/

9. Cleveland Clinic. (2025b, February 20). Everything you need to know about habit stacking for self-improvement. https://health.cleve-landclinic.org/habit-stacking

Chapter 8

1. Calderone, A., Latella, D., Impellizzeri, F., De Pasquale, P., Famà, F., Quartarone, A., & Calabrò, R. S. (2024). Neurobiological changes induced by mindfulness and meditation: A systematic review. *Biomedicines, 12*(11), 2613. https://doi.org/10.3390/biomedicines12112613

2. Yang, Y., Raine, A., Narr, K. L., Colletti, P., & Toga, A. W. (2009). Localization of deformations within the amygdala in individuals with psychopathy. *Archives of General Psychiatry, 66*(9), 986. https://doi.org/10.1001/archgenpsychia-try.2009.110

3. Da Cunha-Bang, S., Fisher, P. M., Hjordt, L. V., Perfalk, E., Skibsted, A. P., Bock, C., Baandrup, A. O., Deen, M., Thomsen, C., Sestoft, D. M., & Knudsen, G. M. (2017). Violent offenders respond to provocations with high amygdala and striatal reactivity. *Social Cognitive and Affective Neuroscience, 12*(5), 802–810. https://doi.org/10.1093/scan/nsx006

Chapter 9

1. Miami City Ballet. (n.d.). Impromptu. https://www.miamicityballet.org/tickets-and-events/impromptu/

2. Legare, C. H., & Nielsen, M. (2020a). Ritual explained: Interdisciplinary answers to Tinbergen's four questions. *Philosophical Transactions of the Royal Society B: Biological Sciences, 375*(1805), 20190419. https://doi.org/10.1098/rstb.2019.0419

Chapter 10

1. CLADglobal.com. (n.d.). Remedy Place opens third location as social wellness trend accelerates. *Architecture and Design News*. https://www.cladglobal.com/CLADnews/architecture_design/Dr-Jonathan-Leary-welcomes-the-growing-momentum-of-social-wellness-as-third-

Remedy-Place-is-launched/354443?source=related

2. Remedy Place. (n.d.). Remedy Place: The world's first social wellness club. https://www.remedy-place.com/

3. Global Wellness Institute. (2024, December 10). Wellness real estate market reached $438 billion in 2023 and is forecast to more than double to $913 billion by 2028. https://globalwellnessinstitute.org/press-room/press-releases/wellness-real-estate-market-reached-438-billion-in-2023-and-is-forecast-to-more-than-double-to-913-billion-by-2028/

4. Global Wellness Institute. (2025, March 25). Wellness communities & real estate trends for 2025. https://globalwellnessinstitute.org/global-wellness-institute-blog/2025/03/25/wellness-communities-real-estate-trends-for-2025/

Chapter 11

1. Japan National Tourism Organization. (n.d.). Forest bathing in Japan (shinrin-yoku). *Travel Japan*. https://www.japan.travel/en/guide/forest-bathing/

2.   Akasawa Natural Recreation Forest, the birthplace of shinrinyoku. (n.d.). https://shinrinyoku.kiso-hinoki.jp/

3.   Highland Quietlife Forest Bathing. (n.d.). Highland QuietLife Forest Bathing. https://www.visitscotland.com/info/see-do/highland-quietlife-forest-bathing-p2502701

4.   Costa Rica Forest Therapy. (n.d.). Forest bathing. https://www.terapiadebosqueynaturaleza.com/us/index.html

5.   Merola, N. (2023, December 20). Morikami Museum: A tranquil forest bathing retreat. *South Florida Digest*. https://southfloridadigest.com/morikami-museum-a-tranquil-forest-bathing-retreat/

6.   Roji-en. (n.d.). Morikami Museum and Japanese Gardens. https://morikami.org/roji-en/#designe

7.   Bureau Staff. (2023, January 25). Forest bathing in the Redwoods. https://www.visitredwoods.com/articles/post/forest-bathing-in-the-redwoods/

8.   Himrod, C. (2021, June 22). The forest within: Finding wisdom in the woods. *Alaska Wilderness League*. https://alaskawild.org/blog/the-forest-within-finding-wisdom-in-the-woods/

9. Liu, Z. (2024). Using roof gardens to alleviate urbanization problems: A case study of Chengdu city. *Applied and Computational Engineering, 58*(1), 85–93. https://doi.org/10.54254/2755-2721/58/20240698

10. Harvard Health. (2019, July 1). A 20-minute nature break relieves stress. https://www.health.harvard.edu/mind-and-mood/a-20-minute-nature-break-relieves-stress

11. Beyer, K., Kaltenbach, A., Szabo, A., Bogar, S., Nieto, F., & Malecki, K. (2014). Exposure to neighborhood green space and mental health: Evidence from the Survey of the Health of Wisconsin. *International Journal of Environmental Research and Public Health, 11*(3), 3453–3472. https://doi.org/10.3390/ijerph110303453

12. Sudimac, S., Sale, V., & Kühn, S. (2022). How nature nurtures: Amygdala activity decreases as the result of a one-hour walk in nature. *Molecular Psychiatry, 27*(11), 4446–4452. https://doi.org/10.1038/s41380-022-01720-6

Chapter 12

1. Living in Design. (n.d.). Achieving wellness: Feng shui & Kanso interiors. https://www.livingindesign.com/journal/interior-design-feng-shui-vs-

kanso

2. So, A. T. P., Lee, E., Li, K. L., & Leung, D. K. S. (2015). Luo shu. *SAGE Open, 5*(2), 215824401558582. https://doi.org/10.1177/2158244015585828

3. Feng Shui Institute International. (n.d.). Feng shui compass luo pan. https://www.feng-shui-institute.org/Feng_Shui/luopan.html

4. World Bank Group. (n.d.). Open Knowledge Repository. https://openknowledge.worldbank.org/entities/publication/f90acc3d-b3d5-5722-b08f-c527c0e3e853

5. UNI. (n.d.). Journal. https://uni.xyz/journal/nice-headquarters-brazil-redefining-sust

6. Futurarc, A. (2021, December 15). Brazil's favelas: A model for green architecture and sustainable living. *FuturArc.* https://www.futurarc.com/commentary/brazils-favelas-a-model-for-green-architecture-and-sustainable-living/

7. Reid, S., & Portilho, G. (2022, April 20). In a São Paulo favela, a former landfill is becoming a public park—Meet the 27-year-old resident behind it.

Vogue. https://www.vogue.com/article/fazendin-hando-park-jardim-colombo-sao-paulo

8. Futurarc, A. (2021, December 15). Brazil's favelas: A model for green architecture and sustainable living. *FuturArc*. https://www.futurarc.com/commentary/brazils-favelas-a-model-for-green-architecture-and-sustainable-living/

9. La Biennale di Venezia. (2021, December 13). Homepage 2021. https://www.labiennale.org/en/architecture/2021

10. Baratto, R. (2018, August 2). The cartographies of the Brazilian Pavilion at the Venice Biennale 2018. *ArchDaily*. https://www.archdaily.com/898893/the-cartographies-of-the-brazilian-pavilion-at-the-venice-biennale-2018

11. Paul Montie Design. (n.d.). MIT Media Lab. https://www.montie.net/work/housing-exhibition

12. MIT Press. (2024, June 18). Book details. https://mitpress.mit.edu/9780262043960/the-world-as-an-architectural-project/

13. Kozlowski, G., Meneguetti, M., & Altberg, A. (2019). 8 reações para o depois: 8 reactions for afterwards.

14. POLES – Political Ecology of Space. (n.d.). Create. https://poles.studio/

Chapter 13

1. UNESCO World Heritage Centre. (n.d.). Historic sanctuary of Machu Picchu. https://whc.unesco.org/en/list/274/

2. Machu Picchu Gateway. (2024, September 11). Machu Picchu walk: Explore the ancient Inca Trail. *Machu Picchu Gateway*. https://www.machupicchu.org/machu-picchu-walk-explore-the-ancient-inca-trail.htm

3. Administración. (2024, April 15). Nazca Lines images. *Peru Travel Blog | Machu Travel Peru*. https://www.machutravelperu.com/blog/nazca-lines-images

4. Newgrange World Heritage Site: Boyne Valley, Ireland. (n.d.). https://www.newgrange.com/

5. Discovering Ancient Egypt. (2024, September 1). Karnak Temple. https://discoveringegypt.com/karnak-temple/

6. Ancient Egypt Magazine. (2024, April 17). Precise construction of funerary structures at Qubbet el-Hawa (Aswan). *The Past*. https://the-

past.com/feature/precise-construction-of-funerary-structures-at-qubbet-el-hawa-aswan/

7. U.S. National Park Service. (n.d.). Pueblo Bonito – Chaco Culture National Historical Park. https://www.nps.gov/chcu/planyourvisit/pueblobonito.htm

8. Chichen Itza. (n.d.). 8 reasons to explore Chichén Itzá. https://www.chichenitza.com/blog/8-reasons-to-explore-chichen-itza

9. Heritage Malta. (2025, February 26). Ħaġar Qim and Mnajdra Archaeological Park. https://heritagemalta.mt/explore/hagar-qim-and-mnajdra-archaeological-park/

10. English Heritage. (n.d.). Stonehenge. https://www.english-heritage.org.uk/visit/places/stonehenge/

11. English Heritage. (n.d.-b). Woodhenge. https://www.english-heritage.org.uk/visit/places/woodhenge/

12. Betz, E. (2023, May 18). Nabta Playa: The world's first astronomical site was built in Africa and is older than Stonehenge. *Astronomy Magazine.* https://www.astronomy.com/observing/nabta-playa-the-worlds-first-astronomical-site-was-built-in-africa-and-is-older-than-stonehenge/

13. Camino de Santiago. (2024, August 12). Camino de Santiago. https://santiago-compostela.net/

14. Follow the Camino. (2024, September 30). Camino Frances. https://followthe-camino.com/en/camino-tours/camino-frances/

Chapter 14

1. Yale University. (2020, August 4). The science of well-being. *Coursera*. https://www.coursera.org/learn/the-science-of-well-being

2. University of Minnesota. (n.d.). Integrative health and medicine. *Coursera*. https://www.coursera.org/specializations/integrative-health-and-medicine

3. Mindvalley. (n.d.). Free meditation for super performance masterclass. https://www.mindvalley.com/mword/masterclass

4. Moughty, S. (2015, November 20). HEAT. *Frontline*. https://www.pbs.org/wgbh/frontline/documentary/heat/

5. Plant, S. (n.d.). The sacred plant. https://the-sacredplant.com/

6. Axe, J. (n.d.). YouTube channel. https://www.youtube.com/channel/UCgtp61tf9tYF7nG_gIQ94LQ/about

7. The Mindful Movement. (n.d.). YouTube channel. https://www.youtube.com/c/TheMindfulMovement

8. The Model Health Show. (2023, October 13). Home. https://themodelhealthshow.com/

9. Wellness Mama. (2025, April 23). Episode archive. https://wellnessmama.com/podcast/

10. Rich Roll. (n.d.). Podcast. https://www.richroll.com/all-episodes/

11. The On Being Project. (2024, October 9). On Being with Krista Tippett. https://onbeing.org/series/podcast/

12. The Mindful Kind. (n.d.). Spotify podcast. https://open.spotify.com/show/5O5tlazpUSpflbc1jAY0ci

13. The Ultimate Health Podcast. (n.d.). https://ultimatehealthpodcast.com/

14. Richardson, C. (2020, January 31). *The art of extreme self-care*. https://cherylrichard-son.com/books/the-art-of-extreme-self-care/

15. Longo, V. (2024, November 19). *The longevity diet*. https://valterlongo.com/the-longevity-diet/

16. Institute for Integrative Nutrition. (n.d.). Webinars. https://www.integrativenutrition.com/webinars

17. Gaia, Inc. (n.d.). Search results for wellness and self-growth webinars. https://www.gaia.com/search?q=wellness%20and%20self%20growth%20webinars

18. Neff, K. (2024, August 27). Self-compassion: Books by Kristin Neff. https://self-compassion.org/books-by-kristin-neff/

19. Barnes & Noble. (n.d.). *The art of happiness* (10th anniversary ed.). https://www.barnesandnoble.com/w/the-art-of-happiness-10th-anniversary-edition-dalai-lama/1100315746

20. Pollan, M. (2024, May 2). *How to change your mind*. https://michaelpollan.com/books/how-to-change-your-mind/

21. Buettner, D. (2023, August 29). Recipes & scientific reporting on Blue Zone food.

https://danbuettner.com/books/blue-zones-solution/

22. Sternberg, E. M. (2009). *Healing spaces: The science of place and well-being*. Harvard University Press.

23. mindbodygreen. (n.d.). Well-rounded well-being for a life well lived. https://www.mindbodygreen.com/

24. Wells, K. (2021, December 8). Blog. *Wellness Mama*. https://wellnessmama.com/blog/

25. University of California, Berkeley. (n.d.). BerkeleyX: The science of happiness. *edX*. https://www.edx.org/learn/happiness/university-of-california-berkeley-the-science-of-happiness

26. HealthUnlocked. (n.d.). The social network for health. https://healthunlocked.com/

27. Association of the United States Army. (2025, March 11). Hot topic: Holistic health and the resilient soldier. https://www.ausa.org/events/hot-topic/holistic-health-and-resilient-soldier

Chapter 15

1. Function Health. (n.d.). Live 100 healthy years. https://www.functionhealth.com/

2. Hyman, M. (2025, April 23). Mark Hyman, MD: Physician, advocate, educator, podcast host. https://drhyman.com/

3. Cleveland Clinic. (n.d.). Functional medicine. https://my.clevelandclinic.org/departments/functional-medicine

4. The UltraWellness Center. (n.d.). https://www.ultrawellnesscenter.com/

5. GLOW Natural Wellness. (n.d.). About us. https://www.glownaturalwellness.com/pages/team

6. GLOW Natural Wellness. (n.d.). Glow Natural Wellness. https://www.glownaturalwellness.com/

7. Headspace. (n.d.). Meditation and sleep made simple. https://www.headspace.com/

8. Calm. (n.d.). Experience calm. https://www.calm.com/ua-homepage

9. Insight Network, Inc. (n.d.). Insight Timer: #1 free meditation app for sleep, relax & more.

https://insighttimer.com/

10. MyFitnessPal. (n.d.). https://www.myfitness-pal.com/

Chapter 16

1. Walk The Mind. (n.d.). [Facebook group]. https://www.facebook.com/groups/WalkThe-Mind/

2. YoungMinds. (n.d.). YoungMinds: The UK's leading charity fighting for children and young people's mental health. https://www.young-minds.org.uk/

3. ITV News Meridian. (2020, September 30). Fund-raiser of the year: Oliver Bowers is using the power of walking to help others with mental health. https://www.itv.com/news/meridian/2020-09-30/fundraiser-of-the-year-oliver-bowers-is-using-the-power-of-walking-to-help-others-with-mental-health

4. Cinque Ports Football Club. (n.d.). Cinque Ports FC official website. https://www.cinque-portsfc.co.uk/

5. Canterbury Christ Church University. (n.d.). https://www.canterbury.ac.uk/

6. Government of Japan. (2024, February 29). Ikigai: The Japanese secret to a joyful life. https://www.japan.go.jp/ki-zuna/2022/03/ikigai_japanese_secret_to_a_joy-ful_life.html

7. Pursuit of Happiness. (2023, April 10). Viktor Frankl: Happiness and meaning. https://www.pursuit-of-happiness.org/history-of-happiness/viktor-frankl/

ABOUT THE AUTHOR

Helen Sandwick is a dynamic self-help author in the health and wellness genre, devoted to empowering readers on their journey to personal growth and balanced living. With a debut novel that intertwines vivid storytelling and practical self-empowerment, Helen draws on a rich background that spans continents and careers. Originally from Northern Ireland, she brings global inspiration and real-life experience to her deeply personal writing, crafting breakthrough moments that resonate with authenticity.

Helen's adventurous spirit shines through her love for travel and a professional path that began with the British Diplomatic Service, later evolving into influential roles in international IT, infusing her work with fresh perspectives and practical wisdom. Currently based in South Florida, she continues to guide readers toward clarity, purpose, and inner peace, with more transformative projects on the horizon.

Contact Helen On

LinkedIn: https://www.linkedin.com/in/helensandwick